KU-284-094

25P

COMMON MARKET COOKERY

ITALY

by

FANNY CRADOCK

British Broadcasting Corporation and
EP Publishing Limited

Published by the British Broadcasting Corporation,
35 Marylebone High Street, London W1M 4AA and
EP Publishing Limited, East Ardsley, Wakefield, Yorkshire.

ISBN 0 563 12682 5 (BBC)
    0 7158 0399 9 (EP)

First published 1974

© Fanny Cradock 1974

Printed in England by John Blackburn Limited, Leeds

Contents

Pasta and Savoury Pizza

Riso (Rice)

Pesce (Fish)

Pollame e Cacciagione (Poultry and Game)

POINTS TO REMEMBER

Unless otherwise specified 'eggs' indicates standard size throughout; 'flour' automatically implies self-raising flour; 'oil' pure olive oil; 'vinegar' wine vinegar; 'salt' either French *gros sel* or English sea salt; 'pepper' freshly milled black peppercorns; 'vanilla' either vanilla pods or alternatively the French *Vanille Liquide Extrait Pur* by *Aussage* or *Vanille en poudre garantie pur* by *Aussage-Pantin*. Both these are sold in $2\frac{1}{2}''$ high brown bottles, easily recognisable.

When milk is indicated for ordinary day-to-day sauces, soups and real custard we use 'silver topped' milk.

Unless specified as 'unsalted butter' the butter given throughout is the one we use for cooking – a brand marked 'not blended'.

We always use electric mixers. Those who do not can use hand rotary whisks or classic loop whisks provided an increased period is allowed for whipping.

Here is your fluid ounce table: 20 fl. oz. = 1 pint
                            10 fl. oz. = $\frac{1}{2}$ pint
                             5 fl. oz. = $\frac{1}{4}$ pint = 1 English gill
                            35 fl. oz. = approx. 1 litre
                            or $1\frac{3}{4}$ pints (to within a Decimal Fraction)
                            $17\frac{1}{2}$ fl. oz. = $\frac{1}{2}$ litre (to within a Decimal Fraction)

Whenever we refer to whipped cream, we leave choosing between whipping and double cream to you.

References to 'potato flour', signify French packet *Fécule de Pommes de Terre*, obtainable from Harrods, Fortnum and Masons, Selfridges, Jacksons of Piccadilly.

All references to liqueurs, *eau de vies* and brandy mean *from a miniature bottle*. Thus you can build a range gradually without crippling expenditure.

TABLE OF EQUIVALENT GAS/ELECTRIC COOKING TEMPERATURES (Supplied by British Gas)

Gas Mark $\frac{1}{4}$ = approximately 240°F	Gas Mark 5 = approximately 380°F
,, ,, $\frac{1}{2}$ = ,, 265°F	,, ,, 6 = ,, 400°F
,, ,, 1 = ,, 290°F	,, ,, 7 = ,, 425°F
,, ,, 2 = ,, 310°F	,, ,, 8 = ,, 445°F
,, ,, 3 = ,, 335°F	,, ,, 9 = ,, 470°F
,, ,, 4 = ,, 355°F	

OIL TEMPERATURES

Slightly smoking hot = 390°–400°F
Just below slightly smoking hot = 360°–385°F

BUYING INFORMATION

Between Brewer Street and Old Compton Street, Soho and the smaller streets which run off left and right of the latter you can be almost certain to find all the food items itemised in this book of Italian Cookery.

In our experience the widest range of pasta, plus hand-made fresh Ravioli, plus dried beans, Italian cheeses, and many other Italian mainstays can be found at both Parmigiani in Old Compton Street and Lina Stores in Brewer Street. Parmigiani is particularly strong on cheeses and, like the cheese counter at Harrods has a very wide selection indeed, so we in London are assured of easy Italiante food shopping.

It is good to be able to tell you therefore, that, subject to the restrictions of travel-time survival in prime condition, all three will send everything which it is logical to ask for through the post. You have only to write, stating your requirements and requesting C.O.D. This in the case of Harrods is only if you do not have an account.

THE COOKING OF ITALY

The Italians reached the peak of their culinary achievements during the Renaissance. This was when Marie de Medici quit her native land with that never-to-be-forgotten-train of courtiers, gentlewomen in attendance, officials and **Italian chefs!** Nothing galls the French more than to be reminded that it was these chefs, dazzled as they journeyed through the Kitchen Garden and Orchard of Europe which was and is the French countryside, brought their methods to bear upon the infinitely superior and varied produce of France. We instance what is known as the Black Diamond of French Gastronomy, the black truffle, versus the Italian white truffle of Bologna. Nor can or could the Italians compete in terms of fish when their coastlines are solely Adriatic and Mediterranean, whilst those of France run North, West and South, yielding the tremendous contrasts of fish from both cold and warm waters.

The Italians, whose range has always run from A to B in comparison with France's A to Zee, have always been past masters at conjuring up delicacies from their more limited arc of raw materials. They revelled in the abundance France gave to them. The French who are nothing if not practical simply picked the Italians' brains, learned from them and went on from there to become the unquestioned leaders of the Gastronomic world.

The cooking of Italy is essentially regional as a mere glance at the recipe titles in this book will show. *Polenta* is an eloquent example with which to establish this fact. Around the Lago di Como we have been given *Polenta* which looks like a giant bathsponge and can be sliced like cake. In the extreme north, in remote mountain areas, *Polenta* is made in a blackened pot, stirred with a vine twig and then either poured over a scrubbed wooden table – possibly under the shade of a vine canopy – and in the poorest homes the families still gather round with a fork apiece. With this, each one forks *Polenta* up working sides to middle. Only on high days and holidays is a little diced cooked meat and/or dried fruits scattered over this basic food. In some cases regional *Polenta* is poured over a kind of shallow, upturned wicker basket affair and then on Feast Days and family celebrations, the aforementioned chopped meats and dried fruits are scattered overall.

To begin at the beginning, there are grades of this yellow maize flour, some rather coarse and some very finely ground. All is cooked in lightly salted water, stirred in with a stick or wooden spoon and cooked slowly with frequent stirrings. *Polenta* is also used to make *Gnocchi,* poured onto an oiled surface, fairly thinly cut into squares or rectangles, sandwiched with ham and cheese or, while still hot, blended with eggs and grated *Parmesan* cheese. In Milan they make a pie with it, with mushrooms and *Béchamel* Sauce. In Venice it frequently replaces bread while a gorgeous de luxe Bolognese version uses the white truffles of the region with a rich cheese sauce to enhance their *Gnocchi.*

Contrary to popular belief all Italy does not eat vast quantities of spaghetti and pasta. In the north of Italy, Lombardy, Piedmont and the Veneto, rice replaces pasta as the staple farinaceous food. Three-quarters of Italy's entire rice crop is grown in the Po valley where the regular flooding creates ideal conditions.

Other sources of confusion arise over the regional differences in the naming of dishes and also in the ingredient variations which occur region by region. Consider the generic name *Zuppa di Pesce* (Fish Soup). On Capri this will frequently be made with *Tonnetto* rather like a delicate mackerel. In Rome it contains *Morene,* while in Leghorn they use lampreys, and *Zuppa di Pesce* is considered to be a main course dish here and not a soup at all! This is the way which we consider the most delicious of all. Along the Viareggio Coastal strip they make this soup with a shell-fish called *Cacciucco* which we in England liken to a first cousin of a very large prawn. Indeed the Viareggio Coastal strip offers such a variety that in all the better restaurants, a table is given over to a special display which includes sea dates *(Datteri di Mare)* – absolutely gorgeous, as are *Peoci* (mussels) and here we go again, because these are called *Muscoli* in some regions! In Genoa the name for the most superb 'fish soup' is *Burrida; Totani* or *Calamaretti* are both inkfish and a Grey Mullet can be either *Cefalo* or *Muggine* – confusing!

Both Milan and Lombardy are supplied from within their regions with *Gorgonzola* and *Bel Paese* cheeses and the area is likewise famous for its *Pannetone,* a cake made with yeast and containing raisins and glacé fruits. Oddly to us, many a café serves slices of *Pannetone* with breakfast coffee. From here *Risotto alla Milanese* originated, and Lombardy also has its own version of *Minestrone* (probably the best) and that clear soup called *Zuppa Pavese. Ossi Bucchi,* a delicious dish made with shin of veal, is also a regional treasure.

Cremona subscribes *Mostarda* to the collection; this is a spiced and piquant mixture of mustard-flavoured sauce with glacé fruits. It could, possibly, be loosely described as the most distinguished member of the Chutney family. As might be expected stuffed, peeled, halved, cored pears with *Gorgonzola* are found around Lombardy. These are then clapped together again; the name for this acquired taste in food is *Pere Ripiene.*

Roman Cookery boasts among its stars the *Porchetta* (sucking pig) and *Abbacchio* (baby lamb); the latter roasted with rosemary can be memorable, which is more than can be said for the average restaurant *Zuppa Inglese* (Italian trifle) usually so soused in *Strega* – a vicious and pungent alcohol – that even sniffing it makes people reel. When made with great restraint which means a very little *Strega* diluted with sugar syrup and/or sweet Italian white wine *Zuppa Inglese* can be very appealing to the sweet-toothed.

In Florence *Bistecca alla Fiorentina* is an undoubted star. You will also encounter omelettes made with tiny, whole, Italian globe artichokes, *Tortini di Carciofi* and that pudding which resembles a mountain of sugary crispness *Cenci alla Fiorentina.*

When you enter Emilia-Romagna you come to the heart of Italian cookery. Parma is there, whose centre is the town of Langhirano, and Parma ham is a gastronome's delight called properly *Prosciutto di Parma*. Some of the best *Parmesan* Cheese is also made in this area while Ravenna grows the region's supply of delicate asparagus (never forget though that none is better than English!). Eels a-plenty are fished from the Comacchio lagoon. In addition there are the sweet cherries of the Vignola area, one of the best pastas called *Tagliatelle* to which all Emilia-Romagna lay claim for its origin and indeed *Tortellini* too. Wherever you travel hereabouts you will see dangling, red-tied *Provolone* cheese pigs among a vast miscellany of cheeses . . . but let us move on to the Northeast and Venice, so that we can reassert our conviction that this city is the most beautiful in the world.

Old Padua, with its colonnaded shops, lays claim to being the original home of the marrow flower fritter and this appears during the season in every *Fritto Misto* of the region and today of the country. In this context may we please diverge to point out that at least one dish pops up with wearisome repetitiousness along every inch of Italian coastline – *Fritto Misto Mare* which can be the most delectable fish miscellany or a lukewarm assembly of dried-up scraps interspersed with rings of india rubber (undercooked inkfish rings) all swathed in winding sheets of pallid batter; it all depends upon the chef or cook. Vicenza claims the finest turkeys and certainly you will find turkey breasts sold separately in every Venetian poulterers. In this great city and along the region's coastline are found the real Scampi, about which fishy odes could still be composed. The fish dishes like the most famous of Italian rice dishes, *Risi e Bisi alla Veneziana* are a glory and a delight whose scope will be proven to you if you make a single visit to the Venetian fish market area. The remaining list is too enormous for us to quote.

Turning from here to Genoa and Liguria we find special and distinctive flavours deriving from the herbs which grow on the Ligurian hillsides . . . sage, oregano, basil, rosemary and dill to cite some of the most important, but far and away the most extensive cookery is of fish. Emperor Barbarossa had a ruling that any Ligurian vessel journeying to Rome should carry with him a shield heaped with the local mussels. Dolphin fillet frequently appear on both home and restaurant menus – as in Venice and great dishes are made with the small eight-tentacle *Polipetto* (or *Moscardini* or *Fragoline di Mare*!), which are all the names of tender little squid, cooked in Genoa with wine and oil. These when cooked resemble scrumpled, bright pink flowers. Another local delight is a kind of *langouste* which is split, grilled and served with a mayonnaise in which pounded lobster 'coral' or eggs are blended. The local *Ravioli* is likewise exceptional. There is also a *Cima alla Genovese,* Italy's answer to the most gorgeous of Ballotines of Veal; this one is made with eggs and pistachio nuts as well.

In and around Naples, oysters are eaten because they come from the Gulf of Taranto where there is a lagoon fed by both fresh and sea waters in which oysters are grown with great success. From the tidal inlet at Taranto splendid mussels are fished, while throughout the inland areas of Calabria there are a multiplicity of good pasta and vegetable soups about which the Calabrians say . . . 'Soup stays the gnawing pangs of hunger, fills the belly, cleans the teeth, aids the digestion, brings colour to the cheeks and induces sound sleep'. People after our own hearts! We are the sworn enemies of those who claim there is no nourishment in soups. You would be surprised how eminent some of these silly billys have been and still are! Hereabouts you will also find that excellent and simple filling sandwich *Mozzarella in Carrozza* made with bread, *Mozzarella* Cheese and treated like a French *Croque M'sieu* before deep frying. These folk are strong too on what an old cook of our parents called 'hoffal'. As you might expect, aubergines, globe artichokes, that curious contortion of the vegetable world, vegetable spaghetti, every conceivable form of marrow and edible gourd, plus tomatoes and pimentoes are in abundant supply. A Calabrian market is one of the most vividly coloured in Europe. Pizzas abound in this region. There are many clam soups *(Zuppa di Vongole)* along the coastline and beefsteak is treated to tomatoes and garlic for *Bistecca alla Pizzaiola*. Nor must we ever risk your missing the *Gelati* (ice-creams). The Southern Italians perfected the art of making them and Italian ice-cream at its best is quite unbeatable.

Finally a word about the Islands of Sicily and Sardinia and their food. The five million islanders of Sicily and the $1\frac{1}{2}$ millions who inhabit Sardinia are somewhat less volatile than their countrymen from the mainland; they are primarily farmers and fishermen. The waters which surround both islands yield tuna, swordfish, mussels, prawns, grey mullet and squid, whilst Sardinia boasts sardines as well – from which the island took its name! From their mountain streams both obtain a plentiful supply of trout.

Sicilians eat very little meat, and most of what they do have is made into cured sausages; but on Sardinia the natural resources include wild boar, sucking pig and kid. Indeed the ritual of open-air roasting all three on Sardinia is well worth seeing as well as eating the end products. They have two principal methods. One a *furria furria* . . . on the turning spit. First the whole animal, baby lamb as well as the aforementioned boar, pig and young goat are skinned, cleaned and spitted. These spit-rods are so erected as to ensure that the flames never touch the flesh above. The fire is kindled with juniper, olive and other aromatic branches. Thus as the turning proceeds the cooking flesh is impregnated with fuel flavoured aromas.

The second method is called a *carrargiu* or 'in a deep hole'. First a hole is dug; this must be of a greater area than the chosen meat. Then a preliminary wood fire is kindled and allowed to burn down completely. Thus the interior soil is thoroughly dried out. Finally the hole is lined thickly on base and at sides, with sprigs of myrtle. The beast is then laid in, covered with more myrtle, very copiously employed and finally an aromatic wood fire is laid and lit on top. Bread is also a staple Sardinian commodity, plus a huge range of pastas; but it is to Sicily that we turn for truly wonderful puddings and *patisserie*. Unbelievable care and patience is expended upon the icing of vast flat wheels of traditional wedding cake, incorporating the names of both bride and groom in the intricate icing designs.

Sicily also has a heavy yield of citrus fruits and grows many olives as well as Sicilian peas which travel to the leading European markets in each spring. When it comes to ice-cream, all the world knows that Sicilians excel but their *Cassata alla Siciliana* which is not 'ice-cream' as the term is generally understood is not nearly widely enough appreciated.

Finally, to end this very brief summary of some regional Italian dishes on a great note, Sicily grows the grapes from which they produce their fortified wine called *Marsala*. Without this the world would never have had *Zabaione*!

THE ITALIANS AT TABLE

An enormous number of Italian businessmen and women in particular and also students of both sexes, go out to break their fast standing in some slit-alley of a minute café for a gulp of coffee and an all-too-frequently dunked bun ingested with reverberating sucks.

Breakfast generally consists of coffee or coffee and cake or sugary breads. The farther south you go the stronger the coffee becomes until in the southernmost areas tiny cups of black treacle replace what we have come to expect from any cup of coffee whether at breakfast or after a main meal. Experienced travellers always request large cups and additional jugs of boiling water to be served with the coffee. Then they can top up the black treacle . . . and survive to see another day. Veterans always ask for butter too if choosing a bun or fancy bread when their palate craves such an accompaniment. It is never served unless specially requested.

ANTIPASTI

(Hors d'Oeuvre)

PROSCIUTTO DI PARMA CON PERE FRESCHE (Parma Ham with ripe Pears)

Ingredients:

$\frac{1}{4}$ lb. paper-thinly cut raw Parma ham;

3–4 (depending on size) ripe pears.

Method: Peel the pears with a silver knife. Cut each one into 6 slices, remove cores and dip into equal parts strained lemon juice and water to stop discoloration. Set 3–4 pear slices centrally on each small plate, arrange 'leaves' of ham between and serve. This is among the simplest of excellent Italian hors d'oeuvre dishes.

CROSTINI DI LUMACHE (Snail *Croûtons*)

Ingredients:

8 slices from a slim bread *flute* fried golden-brown in butter;

$\frac{1}{2}$ fl. oz. olive oil;

1 oz. finely chopped shallot or onion;

2 cloves crushed garlic;

2 oz. chopped, unskinned mushrooms or their stalks;

1 sprig rosemary;

1 flat teaspoon milled, fresh parsley heads;

salt and pepper;

1 standard tin snails.

Method: Drain snails, slice and fry bread and keep warm. Heat oil, fry onions gently for 3 minutes, stirring and shaking pan. Add garlic, mushrooms, **pounded** rosemary spikes and prepared parsley. Stir well and as mushrooms shrink add snails and turn carefully over low heat for 12 minutes. Then pile pan contents equally over *croûtons*, season lightly with salt, and liberally with black pepper.

CROSTINI DI PROVATURA (Cheese *Croûtons*)

Use *Mozzarella, Bel Paese, Provolone* or *Gruyère* (in that order of precedence).

Ingredients:

Six $\frac{1}{4}''$ thick slices French bread *(flute)*;

6 matching slices of chosen cheese;

6 small or 4 large washed, dried, anchovy fillets;

3 to $3\frac{1}{2}$ oz. melted butter.

Method: Place cheese on bread, set on a heat-resistant serving dish and brown/melt in oven, Gas Mark 6, one shelf above centre, for 6 to 9 minutes. While the bread crisps and cheese melts, chop anchovies pretty finely in a little of their own oil, place for a moment or two over low flame in the hot melted butter and pour overall at moment of service.

CROSTINI DI MARE (Seafood *Croûtons*)

Ingredients:

6/8 fried *croûtons* (see *Crostini di Muscoli* p. 16);

1 oz. butter;

1 small, crushed garlic clove;

$\frac{1}{2}$ fl. oz. olive oil;

1 scant teaspoon finely chopped fennel;

black pepper;

3 oz. shelled shrimps;

1 fillet of sole or plaice weighing 3 oz.;

1 dessertspoon strained lemon juice;

1 oz. finely chopped onion or shallot.

Method: Dissolve butter with oil and when both 'sing' fry onions gently for 4 minutes, stirring and shaking to avoid onions sticking. Add garlic, fennel, and chosen white fish cut into short, slim strips. Turn again while cooking until fish strips stiffen and lose all transparency. Stir in shrimps, season with pepper, add lemon juice, stir again and divide between *croûtons*.

CROSTINI DI FEGATINI (Liver *Croûtons*)

Ingredients:

8 oz. chickens' livers;

1 large slice lean, cooked, diced small ham;

2–3 oz. butter depending upon size of livers;

salt and pepper to season;

½ medium lemon;

flour;

3 tablespoons stock;

six ¼″ thick slices French bread fried in butter.

Method: Dice livers and turn lightly in flour. Dissolve 2 oz. butter in shallow pan, brown ham diced lightly, add livers and cook very gently for 3 minutes. Add stock, generous pinch pepper, small pinch salt, and shake and stir over gentle heat until it is well blended. Reduce heat to mere thread, cover and allow a further 6 to 7 minutes. Heap on to *crostini*, squeeze lemon juice lightly over all and serve immediately.

CROSTINI DI MUSCOLI (Mussel *Croûtons*)

Fry six ¼″ French bread slices in butter. Scrub, beard, steam until opened and remove from shell, 4 pints of mussels. Place in pan with 1 crushed garlic clove, 2 heaped tablespoons milled parsley heads and 10 fl. oz. dry white *Chianti*. Bubble fiercely for 1 minute, remove mussels, heap on to *crostini* breads, continue bubbling liquor until slightly syrupy, pour over all and serve immediately.

CROSTINI DI ARANCI FREDDI
(Orange *Crostini* with Cheese)

These cold *crostini* are perfectly delicious and very refreshing in hot weather. We prefer to recommend as a base the quite unorthodox use of German black bread of the kind sold at the German Centre in Knightsbridge. It comes in ready-sliced long-keeping packs. Correctly speaking, *crostini* should be made of thickly buttered rounds of long narrow bread *flutes*.

Ingredients:

6/8 bread rounds;

butter;

½ lb. Italian *Stracchino* or cream cheese;

2 oz. shelled walnuts (dried) – but in season try it with peeled fresh ones;

the heart of 1 (any) available lettuce;

salt and pepper;

2/3 oz. red pimento;

6/8 stuffed olives;

2 really juicy thin-skinned oranges.

Method: Wash, drain and tear lettuce; cut lettuce is an abomination and weeps out all its goodness! Lay down as a bed on a shallow serving dish. Place available creamy cheese in a bowl with finely chopped walnuts withholding one half for each chosen bread slice garnish. Work up together with a seasoning of salt and white pepper to taste and spread $\frac{3}{4}$ of this on breads. Peel oranges with a very sharp knife so as to cut both pith and skin away simultaneously, leaving all flesh cleanly exposed. Slide knife down just inside skin of 1 segment and repeat on opposing side, being careful to remove all pips. Do this over a small bowl to catch inevitable oozing juice. After first slice just make first cut downwards then turn (pointed) knife and jerk out all other segments. Arrange, overlapping, in a circle on cream and nut spread. Put small blob or piped rosette of remaining cheese mixture in the centre of each. Surmount with a $\frac{1}{2}$ walnut on each peak. Stab a wooden cocktail stick with a stuffed olive and stab at an angle just outside each central cheese peak. Slice up remainder and scatter over lettuce bed, and shake all saved orange juice, after squeezing out juice fruit-denuded skins, over all.

OLIVE RIPIENE (Stuffed Olives)

For these we recommend you contact the Trade Section of the American Embassy to obtain current stockists of large tinned, stoned, green olives which the Americans call 'pitted olives'. They are excellent but stockists are too variable to justify naming them as constant sources!

Ingredients for stuffing:

1 fl. oz. olive oil;

1 oz. butter;

4 oz. raw, minced, white meat of chicken;

2 oz. lean, minced raw ham (or gammon);

1 oz. *Parmesan* cheese;

a generous pinch of nutmeg;

salt, pepper and 1 very small egg;

possibly a few fine, soft breadcrumbs.

Method: Dissolve butter with oil in a small thick pan and when both 'sing', stir in the ham and chicken and cook gently for 4 to a maximum of 5 minutes. Remove from heat, season with salt and black pepper, add nutmeg and cheese and when cooled down just a little beaten egg and beat in quickly and thoroughly. If too runny a mixture is thus obtained, just bring back to a nice piping consistency with fine breadcrumbs, scattered over and beaten in. Place in a nylon (non-sweat) icing bag with a $\frac{1}{4}''$ writing pipe affixed and pipe into the hollows of the large, stoned olives. Pile in a pyramid on one d'oyley covered dish or, if preferred, spike each one with a small (wooden) cocktail stick.

MELONE E FICHI (Melon with Figs)

This is a description and not a recipe!

For this dish the melon slices are cut very thinly and the rind is generally removed after de-pipping and pithing. These slices or crescents are then arranged like the petals of a flower on each plate and ripe green figs are quartered down from the tips to the fat ends (but not right through) until they too can be opened like flowers. Then one is set centrally to form the heart of each melon 'flower', and the remaining full-quartered ones are set between the spaces made by the melon petals. Alternatively, and more simply, a fat slice of de-pipped and pithed melon is set on one side of each plate and 2, 3 or even 4 figs are set on the opposite side of the plate. In which case each person quarters the figs as already described.

MELONE E PROSCIUTTO DI PARMA
(Melon with Parma Ham)

See previous recipe and merely replace figs with very thin slices raw Parma ham.

CRESPOLINI (Stuffed Pancakes)

Ingredients:

6 thin pancakes;

3 oz. (cooked weight) sieved spinach (see p. 68);

1 small egg;

2 oz. chicken's (or duck's) liver;

1 oz. butter;

2½ oz. *Ricotta* or cream cheese;

2½ oz. finely grated *Parmesan* cheese;

½ pint thick white sauce;

salt and black pepper to season;

1 oz. *Mozzarella* or *Bel Paese* cheese.

Method: Mix *Ricotta* or cream cheese with prepared spinach, beat in egg and 1 oz. of given *Parmesan*. Add a small nut of the butter, a tablespoon of the thick white sauce and the chosen livers, first fried for a few minutes in the remaining butter. Drain, chop and fold into the rest. Reserve the remaining pan butter. Butter a shallow heat-resistant dish, season to taste with salt and pepper and then pour in remaining white sauce. Level off. Divide made filling between the pancakes equally. Roll up in cylinders and lay over sauce. If preferred these may each be cut slantwise into 3 before putting in position. Slice the *Mozzarella* or *Bel Paese* extremely thinly, lay over pancakes, scatter remaining *Parmesan* overall, moisten with melted pan butter (from cooking the livers) and bake briskly, 1 shelf above centre at Gas Mark 6 for 12–15 minutes or until cheese is bubbling and golden brown.

TONNO E SALSA TONNATA

(Tuna Fish with Tuna Sauce)

Ingredients:

8 oz. tinned tuna fish (*Salsa di tonna* p. 86);

1 heart of lettuce;
12 little black olives.

Method: Tear chosen lettuce, arrange on shallow dish. Break tuna into neat pieces conserving oil in tin. Mask with given sauce, and decorate with olives.

UOVA E SALSA AGRODOLCE

(Egg Sweet/Sour Sauce)

Ingredients:

6 eggs;

Salsa Agrodolce (p. 87).

Method: Slide eggs gently into well-bubbling boiling water. Maintain for exactly 4 minutes. Have ready a bowl of cold water. Slide in eggs-in-shell after boiling. Tap shells all over to crack, then hold each one in turn under a thin stream of cold water from tap. Pick a scrap of shell away and thereafter water will force top shell and under-skin away sufficiently for you to peel away remainder without breaking open fragile poached eggs. Slice a scrap from the broad base of each egg. Stand on a dish and pour *Salsa Agrodolce* over all.

MINESTRE

(Soup)

PAPAROT (Spinach Soup)

This is one of the most delicious soups to come out of Italy.

Ingredients:

1 lb. (picked weight) well-washed and drained, fresh spinach;

2½ oz. salted butter;

1 large, peeled, crushed garlic clove;

1 generous pinch nutmeg;

2 rounded tablespoons semolina;

1 heaped tablespoon flour;

2½ pints water;

½ pint milk;

grated *Parmesan* cheese;

salt and pepper.

Method: Place drained, but not dried, spinach leaves with ½ oz. butter in a thick pan. Set over low heat and allow to draw in own juices and subside. Cook for maximum 7 minutes. Dissolve remaining butter in a separate (large-ish) pan. Stir in flour to form a fluid *roux,* add the spinach (undrained), the prepared garlic, 1 flat teaspoon of salt and 1 flat eggspoon of pepper. Work in water gradually with a wooden spoon and allow to come to boiling point. Maintain for 2 to 3 minutes then work in the semolina, sprinkling it over surface and stirring it in. Cook for 30 minutes over very moderate heat and with an occasional stir. Emulsify or liquidise. Return to pan, add nutmeg and milk, stir until boiling. Taste, correct seasoning as desired and serve immediately or chill and re-heat for service as required, handing grated cheese separately.

MINESTRONE (Mixed Vegetable)

Ingredients:

3–4 parsley stalks;

4 oz. white haricot beans, overnight soaked in cold water;

4 finely chopped medium onions;

2–3 peeled crushed garlic cloves;

3 oz. de-rinded streaky bacon or diced raw lean ham;

6–8 bacon rinds;

4 oz. very thinly sliced raw tight white cabbage;

2 finely chopped celery hearts;

1 *bouquet garni;*

1 large diced raw potato;

4 medium or 6 small ripe tomatoes;

4 fl. oz. water;

generous pinch nutmeg;

a generous pinch of basil;

3 oz. crushed *Vermicelli;*

6 oz. diced green beans;

2 medium leeks chopped finely;

grated *Parmesan* cheese;

salt and pepper to season;

plenty of good bone stock.

Method: Strain the white beans and place in a very roomy pan with the parsley stalks and prepared onions, garlic cloves, bacon or ham, bacon rinds, cabbage, celery hearts, potato, green beans and leeks. Cover liberally with clear bone stock. Bring to a slow rolling boil. Remove the inevitable scum which forms on the top. Refresh with $\frac{1}{2}$ a tumbler of cold water and steady off at a slow simmer. Cook for $2\frac{1}{2}$ hours. Meanwhile, skin and rough-cut the tomatoes. Place in a very small pan with $\frac{1}{2}$ pint of stock. Simmer until tender. Add the generous pinch of basil (fresh or dry) and the nutmeg, rub through a sieve and add at end of given cooking time to the soup in the pan. Also add the *Vermicelli.* Cook for a very few moments until this is *al dente* or firm to the teeth. Correct seasoning with salt and pepper and serve.

Note: Because you virtually eat rather than drink this soup with liberal sprinklings of given *Parmesan* cheese (handed separately) we break our normal rule and suggest you use well-heated deepish bowls or soup plates.

Note: This soup re-heats beautifully, and if it over-thickens merely add more stock and bring to the boil before serving.

RAVIOLI IN BRODO (Clear Soup with Pasta)

Ingredients:

Given quantity of *Ravioli* (p. 26);   3 pints *Consommé* (p. 22).

Method: Heat *Consommé.* Immerse made, divided *Ravioli* and poach at gentle simmer for 4–5 minutes. Pour all into a heated tureen and serve in heated soup bowls.

Beef Consommé

Ingredients:

2 lb. lean stewing beef;

1 large carrot;

1 large Spanish onion;

1 outside white stem of celery;

2 quarts cold water;

gros sel or rock salt and black pepper.

Method: Place the piece of beef, lengthwise quartered carrot, quartered onion and celery stem cut into 1″ pieces, into a roomy saucepan. Cover with cold water. Bring to the boil slowly. When boiling reduce bottom heat to a mere thread, skin off all surplus scum which forms on the top until you can see pan contents clearly. Cover, raise heat just sufficiently to obtain a gentle simmer and maintain for at least 6 hours. Strain and chill. Remove all fat from the surface. Taste and correct seasoning with salt and freshly milled black pepper.

ZUPPA PAVESE (Clear Soup with Eggs)

Ingredients:

2½ pints clear, strongly reduced chicken, meat or vegetable stock;

6 eggs;

18 small squares of bread;

grated *Parmesan* cheese or substitute hard cheese.

Method: Having reduced the chosen stock until it **really tastes** and while it is hot, poach the eggs in it in a wide shallow pan. Lift them out into heated soup bowls and pour stock over until each is filled, using strainer if you have any threads of egg white floating about in the stock. Fry little pieces of bread, spread grated cheese liberally over them and float 3 around each egg in each bowl. Hand extra cheese separately.

Note: This is a marvellous thing for someone who lives alone as well as for a large family, except that the live-aloner will be compelled to use a small tin of *Consommé* suitably diluted with tap water. When making for 6 people as given in our recipe, please bear one thing in mind. If you use all tap water instead of reduced stock or if you use a *bouillon* cube, that is what it will taste like! The better the stock, the better the soup . . . and the better for **you**.

MINESTRA MILLE FANTI (Cheese Soup)

Ingredients:

2 oz. freshly grated breadcrumbs;

3 oz. grated *Parmesan* cheese;

nutmeg, salt and pepper to season;

2 standard eggs;

1½ pints cleared, well-reduced stock or *Consommé* (p. 22).

Method: Bring the stock or *Consommé* to the boil in a fairly roomy pan and draw to the side of the heat, reducing this to minimum. Mix given cheese and breadcrumbs and beat well with a wooden spoon, adding the 2 eggs singly. Turn mixture into the hot stock or *Consommé*, stir roughly and leave for 15 minutes. Add nutmeg to taste, correct seasoning with salt and pepper, then whisk up vigorously. Bring up to boiling point **but do not boil** and serve immediately.

STRACCIATELLA (Roman Soup with Eggs and Cheese)

This is a simple soup and when well-made is very good indeed but it must be made with really good, flavoursome stock. It is no mortal use thinking that it will taste good with a meat cube and water! Ideally use stock made from carcase, neck, and giblets of a fowl, but any good well-reduced stock will suffice to make it well.

Ingredients:

2 pints strong stock;

2 eggs;

2 oz. grated *Parmesan* cheese;

1 tablespoon fine semolina.

Method: Heat 1½ pints of chosen stock. Whip up the eggs, work in the *Parmesan* and semolina, and dilute with gradual additions of the remaining ½ pint of cold stock. When the stock being heated reaches boiling point, stir egg mixture with a fork and with the other hand pour hot stock gradually onto the egg mixture. Return to pan when all is blended and reheat soup to just below boiling point. Serve immediately.

Note: Please do not worry that egg mixture goes into little flakes throughout the soup. It is meant to!

ZUPPA DI CASTAGNE (Chestnuts)

We have deliberately made this as easy as possible for you by a little cheating and the recommendation of Clement Faugier's chestnut *purée*, sold in any good Soho grocers and also by Harrods, Fortnum and Mason, Selfridges in London, under its French title on one side of the tin – *Purée de Marrons Nature* – and on the other side Fresh Chestnut *Purée*.

Ingredients:

One 15½ oz. tin chestnut *purée*;

3 oz. diced bacon fat;

6 oz. peeled-weight onions;

4 oz. scraped red of carrots, also chopped;

1 celery heart, chopped extremely finely;

3½ pints stock, chicken or pork, but if you should happen to have the carcase of a duck handy, this would be perfection!;

salt and pepper to season.

Method: Place bacon fat dice in a thick frying pan over a very low heat and allow the fat to run and the dice to shrivel up and become dark brown. Then remove the shrivelled dice. The easiest way to do this is with a perforated spoon. Into the pan fat, heated again, slide in the finely chopped onions, carrots and celery and fry over a moderate heat for 5 minutes. Work in the chestnut *purée* very thoroughly. Work in the stock gradually, simmer with frequent stirrings for 12–15 minutes and serve with slices of Italian rolls fried until brown and nicely crisp in more bacon fat or unsalted raw pork fat, either of which must previously have been rendered down.

ZUPPA CREMA DI POLLO (Chicken and Egg)

The quality of this soup depends upon the reduction of a larger than given quantity of stock made with the smashed-down carcase, liver and giblets of a chicken, reduced down to a well-flavoured stock.

Ingredients:

3 pints strongly reduced chicken stock;

2 eggs;

the juice of 1 large lemon;

8 fl. oz. best possible milk;

2 oz. ground rice;

2 thin slices of cooked chicken breast cut into *allumettes* or matchsticks;

nutmeg, salt and black pepper to season.

Method: Put the given quantity of strongly flavoured stock into a roomy pan and allow to heat to boiling point. Work the ground rice with the cold milk to make a smooth, runny paste. Pour on to this paste a little boiling stock, stir again, scrape into pan, stir thoroughly over a low heat (ideally with pan set over an asbestos mat) and allow to cook with occasional further stirrings for 25 minutes. Work in the lemon juice, then the nutmeg, salt and pepper to taste. Strain through a *tamis* or very fine ordinary strainer. Return to low heat and re-heat through. Break eggs into a bowl, whip them very thoroughly. Pour on some of the hot soup, stir well, return to soup pan and stir again, but on no account allow mixture to boil or eggs will curdle. Pour into heated tureen for service, stir in chicken *allumettes* and send to table.

MINESTRA DI POMODORI FREDDI
(Cold Tomato)

Ingredients:

2 lb. rough-chopped, skinned, ripe tomatoes;

2 fl. oz. olive oil;

1 medium, peeled, crushed garlic clove;

1 rounded teaspoon freshly milled parsley heads;

1 flat teaspoon finely chopped basil leaves;

1½ pints good, well-reduced stock;

salt and pepper to season;

a generous pinch of castor sugar.

Method: Heat oil, add the prepared tomatoes, garlic, parsley and basil. Simmer gently for about 6 minutes with an occasional stir. Work in the given stock and the sugar, season to taste with salt and pepper. Simmer on for a further 5 minutes, rub through a sieve. Pour into a jug or other suitable container and refrigerate until very cold indeed. Serve in bowls with an additional pinch of chopped fresh basil dropped over the top of each serving.

Note: The character of this soup is entirely changed, but becomes absolutely delicious when transformed into *Crema di Pomodori Freddi* (see below).

CREMA DI POMODORI FREDDI
(Cold Cream of Tomato)

Please turn to *Minestra di Pomodori Freddi* (above) and make exactly as the given recipe. The additional requirements are:

3 fl. oz. single or coffee cream;

3 fl. oz. yoghurt;

6 ice cubes.

When the soup is cold, stir in the cream and yoghurt. At the moment of service pour into bowls, drop an ice cube in each and sprinkle lightly overall with additional finely chopped basil leaves.

PASTA AND SAVOURY PIZZA

RAVIOLI

Ingredients:

8 oz. sifted flour;

2 oz. butter;

1 scant level teaspoon salt and approximately $\frac{1}{2}$ a teacup of cold water.

Method: Sift salt and flour together into a roomy bowl. Rub in butter very finely with fingertips and bind to a good, rolling paste, working in water with a small table knife. Turn paste onto a cold, floured, working surface (ideally marble). Dust over all with flour and knead paste for about 3 minutes. Place in a floured cloth and refrigerate for a minimum of 30 minutes. Divide paste into 2 parts of $5\frac{1}{2}$ oz. and $7\frac{1}{2}$ oz. and roll larger piece out very thinly indeed on a lightly floured, cold working surface. Roll up paste over floured rolling pin and unroll onto a sheet of lightly floured greaseproof paper. Dust top-surface of this paste panel lightly with flour. Cover with a second sheet of greaseproof. Repeat rolling instructions with smaller piece of paste and trim edges to form a neat rectangle. Brush top surface all over very thoroughly with raw, beaten, strained whole egg. Filling can be made very accurate and very easy IF you draw a checkerboard of $1\frac{3}{4}''$ squares with a pencil onto greaseproof paper. Place this over the trimmed panel of pastry. Prick the centre of each square with a skewer. Remove. Pipe chosen filling centrally over each skewer-mark using a nylon icing bag with a plain $\frac{1}{4}''$ writing pipe affixed. This makes a neat $\frac{1}{2}''$ blob each time, leaving the requisite margin all round for the eventual cutting up of finished *Ravioli* into $1\frac{3}{4}''$ squares. Brush under side of larger piece of rolled-out pastry with cold water and lay over filling-dotted rectangle. Press paste down firmly with clean finger-tip between dabs of filling. Trim surplus from edges of top layer of paste and then cut up the *Ravioli* easily and quickly with a knife. Refrigerate until required.

BEEF FILLING FOR RAVIOLI

Ingredients:

6 oz. minced, cold, cooked beef;

6 oz. cooked spinach;

2 oz. cooked, sieved brains (classic) or cream cheese (a reasonable substitute);

1 rounded dessertspoon finely chopped or grated carrot or

onion (poached for 4 minutes in a very small amount of hot butter);

2 oz. grated *Parmesan* cheese;

1 egg;

pinches of salt and pepper and nutmeg to season.

Method: Mix all together, beat well and pipe out as instructed.

CHEESE FILLING FOR RAVIOLI

Ingredients:

4 oz. cooked spinach;

4 oz. *Ricotta,* cream or cottage cheese;

1 oz. grated *Parmesan;*

pinches of salt, pepper and nutmeg to season plus 1 scant teaspoon of either basil or marjoram.

Method: Mix all together and pipe out as instructed.

How to Cook Ravioli

Cook *Ravioli* in fast-boiling salted water (1 oz. to 5 pints) or use slightly salted stock. Cooking time 4–5 minutes, by which time all the little *Ravioli* will have risen to the top.

Final Assembly

1. Drain, pile into a dish and hand a bowl of grated *Parmesan* and a small sauceboat of melted butter separately, or,

2. Drain, place in a liberally buttered heat-resistant dish in layers with sprinklings of grated *Parmesan* cheese in between. Cover last layer with a liberal sprinkling of cheese. Add a few small butter flakes and cook at Gas Mark 4, centre shelf, until piping hot, or,

3. Serve with grated *Parmesan* cheese and Tomato Sauce.

HOW TO MAKE LASAGNE VERDI

(Green Noodles)

Ingredients:

1 lb. flour;

3 eggs;

3 oz. (uncooked weight) spinach
purée;

2 flat teaspoons salt.

Method: Sift flour onto cold surface, gather fingers into posy and push out from centre to form a ring. Place in the centre, the eggs, the well pressed spinach *purée* and the salt. Then work up with a small table knife in each hand. When paste is assembled knead as with bread dough, pushing away from you with the thumb pad or 'heel' of your hand until the paste has considerable elasticity; this will take between 9 and 10 minutes. Divide the paste into 2 pieces. Dust a cold working surface with sifted flour, rub rolling pin with flour and roll out the dough, pulling it thinner and thinner all the time and very lightly flour the paste as you roll so as to ensure it will not stick. When you have rolled and pulled it to such an extent that it is firm enough to fold up without fear of splitting or crack-ing, repeat this procedure with second piece. Then roll up each piece separately and cut into ½″ wide strips. Toss into roomy pan of fast boiling slightly salted water and cook for 5 minutes. Drain and place in roomy bowl filled with cold slightly salted water, lift out each piece, pat dry and use.

LASAGNE VERDI (Green Noodles)

Ingredients:

1 batch *Lasagne Verdi* (green
  pasta);

1 pint thick, white sauce with
  additional flavouring of a pinch
  of nutmeg;

a little butter;

grated *Parmesan* cheese;

1 batch *Ragù Bolognese* (p. 83).

Method: Three-quarters fill a very large saucepan with slightly salted boiling water. When the water bubbles, throw in the *Lasagne*. Stir until the water re-boils, cook for 5 minutes, drain and place in a bowl of cold, salted water. Drain again when cold. Butter a large, deep, heat-resistant dish or in moments of crisis use an ordinary meat baking tin. Then cover the base with a coating of *Ragù Bolognese*. Cover this with a layer of the sauce, then lay down a layer of *Lasagne* and repeat until all ingredients are absorbed, ending with the sauce. Sprinkle the top generously with grated *Parmesan*. Bake on the middle shelf of oven at Gas Mark 5 for 25/30 min-utes and serve piping hot.

LASAGNE E SALSA DI FUNGHI

(Plain Ribbon Noodles with Mushroom Sauce) (*Salsa di Funghi* p. 85).

Lasagne is also the term for several widths of flat, uncoloured noodles – just to confuse you!

Ingredients:

¾ lb. ribbon noodles;

Salsa di Funghi (p. 85);

1 tablespoon olive oil;

grated *Parmesan* cheese.

Method: Cook noodles exactly as for *Lasagne Verdi* (p. 28). Strain, return to dried pan, stir with olive oil. Turn onto a heated dish and pour sauce overall. Hand grated *Parmesan* cheese separately.

LASAGNE FESTONATE E SUGO DI CARNE (Ribbon Pasta, Italian Meat Sauce)

Ingredients:

½–¾ lb. curly-edged ribbon pasta;

Sugo di Carne (p. 84);

1 tablespoon olive oil;

grated *Parmesan* cheese.

Method: Immerse pasta in plenty of salted fast-boiling water. Stir until water re-boils and thereafter allow 11½/12½ minutes maximum unless wanting pasta to be totally over-cooked by Italian standards. Drain, wipe pan, return pasta and stir with olive oil until shiny and thoroughly impregnated. Turn onto a heated dish and scoop out a generous hollow in centre. Turn sauce into this and hand grated *Parmesan* cheese separately.

SPAGHETTI E COZZE (with Mussels)

Ingredients:

1 lb. spaghetti;

3 pints mussels;

salt and pepper to season;

1 small handful fresh sage leaves and a sprig for garnish;

½ pint *Salsa Pizzaiola* (p. 85);

1 lb. fish trimmings;

1 bay leaf;

4 peppercorns;

1 sprig fennel (optional);

1 'leaf' lemon peel;

water;

2 tablespoons olive oil.

Method: Half fill a roomy pan with slightly salted water, toss in spaghetti when water bubbles furiously (which makes the water come off the boil so stir until water re-boils) and then cook for precisely 12 minutes. Meanwhile place fish trimmings, bay leaf, peppercorns and optional fennel with lemon 'leaf' in a pan. Just cover with boiling water. Bring to the boil, simmer for 20 minutes and strain. Reduce strained liquor by simmering to

$\frac{3}{4}$ pint. Mix with the *Salsa Pizzaiola*. Clean and steam the mussels until they are opened. Then, as soon as the mussels are cool enough to handle, remove from shells. Strain spaghetti very thoroughly. Dry the cooking pan equally thoroughly. Return spaghetti to pan, toss in the chopped sage leaves and oil, turn very thoroughly so that spaghetti shines and is well impregnated with oil and herbs. Tip into a dish, make a well in the centre, place all mussels in the sauce, just bring to the boil as they will have cooled off somewhat and pour into centre well. Serve piping hot.

POLENTA (Semolina or Yellow Maize Flour)

This is primarily one of the staple foods of Northern Italy right across Lombardy to the Veneto where it almost invariably appears with little roasted birds like the *Beccafichi* (the vine peckers), but in the mountain areas of Northern Italy there are 2 fascinating variants. The mixture is made up to a pouring consistency and is then poured over a well-scrubbed table, probably under a grape-vine canopy. When in sufficient funds it is then sprinkled with finely chopped cooked sausage and dried fruits. Each member of the family is provided with a fork and they either stand or sit around the table and tuck in, working sides to middle.

Alternatively, there is a very shallow woven basket which is inverted on the table. The mixture is poured over this and then eaten in the same way.

To make: Boil 2 pints well salted water in a roomy pan. Gradually scatter in $\frac{3}{4}$ lb. chosen type *Polenta*, stirring round with either a vine stick or a wooden spoon until thick and smooth. Like this it is pretty depressing fare! Much better is the method of allowing it to get cold on a lightly oiled surface, stamp it out into shapes (as for *Gnocchi*, p. 69). Bake in the oven either as given for *Gnocchi* or with a meat and tomato sauce.

PIZZA ITALIANA

Ingredients:

12 oz. bread dough (p. 31);

2 oz. thinly sliced *Emmenthal* cheese;

3 oz. stoned green olives;

2½ oz. anchovy fillets;

salt, pepper and sweet marjoram to season;

garlic oil (see p. 86);

1 oz. black olives;

concentrated tomato *purée;*

12 capers;

4 small, rough-cut, skinned, de-seeded, tomatoes;

1 skinned, rough-cut, red pimento.

Method: Roll paste into circle approximately $\frac{1}{4}''$ thick. Place on baking sheet, cover base with very finely sliced cheese. Fill gaps in between with $\frac{1}{2}$ the black and green olives cut in small pieces. Divide anchovy fillets lengthwise, chop up $\frac{1}{2}$, curl remainder into little coils. Sprinkle with marjoram, season with salt and pepper. Dot surface with coiled anchovies and use tomato *purée* to pipe a criss-cross trellis over surface. Dot remaining anchovies here and there, cover surface with oil, season liberally with milled black pepper and bake, Gas Mark 6, middle shelf, until paste rim is a good golden brown.

PIZZA ALLA GARIBALDI

(Italian Pizza with Pimentoes)

Ingredients:

12½ oz. bread dough or raw, bought or home-made puff paste;

3½ oz. transparently thinly sliced *Gruyère* or *Emmenthal;*

8 stuffed green olives;

6 coiled anchovy fillets;

pepper;

6 black olives;

1–2 chopped tinned pimentoes cut into narrow strips;

4–5 tablespoons tomato *purée* or 2 rounded dessertspoons concentrated tomato *purée* thinned to spreading consistency with a little cold stock;

3–4 tablespoons olive oil;

1 slightly rounded teaspoon fresh or dried marjoram.

Method: Roll out chosen paste into a circle 8–9″ in diameter and place on a floured baking sheet. Brush all over lightly with extra olive oil. Spread with chosen tomato *purée*. Scatter cheese slices over surface, then stoned, quartered black olives in between. Trellis with pimento strips. Dot surface with stuffed olives and coiled anchovies. Sprinkle with pepper and marjoram. Moisten overall with the oil and bake at Gas Mark 6, 1 shelf above centre, for 25–30 minutes for pastry base at Gas Mark 7, same position, for 15–18 minutes for bread dough. When able and willing to make this at home use 2 separate 1½ lb. of strong white flour, 1 oz. bakers' yeast, 1 oz. castor sugar, 15¾ fl. oz. each of milk and water totalling 31½ fl. oz., 1 oz. salt. Place 1½ lb. flour in warmed mixing bowl. Make hole centrally. Stir yeast with sugar until liquified. Pour into hole. Blend cold milk with water at 98·4°F. Pour over yeast mixture. Work up by hand to loose paste. Work in salt. Cover with thick cloth. Prove in warm place 15–20 minutes. Then add remaining flour, work up by hand to smooth dough and knead for minimum 10 minutes on lightly floured surface. Cut off required quantity for *pizza* (using the bulk for bread). Roll out *pizza* quantity into circle, lay on lightly floured baking sheet, cover lightly and re-prove until dough has doubled its thickness (approx. 25–30 minutes).

CAPPELLETTI E SUGO DI CARNE
(Little Hat-Shaped Pasta in Italian Meat Sauce)

These pasta are sold with the stuffing already inside the tiny 'crowns' of the hats.

Follow the recipe for *Lasagne Festonata* (p. 29) exactly allowing a minute or two less cooking time for the *Cappelletti*.

FARFALLE E RAGÙ BOLOGNESE
(Pasta Bows)

Ingredients:

$\frac{1}{2}$–$\frac{3}{4}$ lb. *Farfalle;*
bowl of grated *Parmesan* cheese.

1 given batch *Ragù Bolognese* (p. 83).

Method: Toss pasta bows into plenty of fast-boiling, well-salted water. Maintain at steady bubbling boil for 8–9 minutes. Drain thoroughly and return to dried saucepan. Cover with *Ragù*, turn well and turn onto heated dish. Hand cheese separately.

CONCHIGLIA/LUMACHE E SALSA GENOVESE (Pasta Shells with Genoese Sauce)

Ingredients:

$\frac{1}{2}$–$\frac{3}{4}$ lb. chosen pasta shells;
1 given batch *Salsa Genovese* (p. 83);

bowl of grated *Parmesan* cheese;
1 tablespoon olive oil.

Method: Cook pasta shells as explained for *Farfalle* (above). Drain and return to dried pan. Toss with oil, form into border on heated dish, pour sauce into centre. Serve and hand cheese separately.

TAGLIATELLE VERDI CON SALSA PIZZAIOLA (Green Noodles with Tomato Sauce)

Ingredients:

3–4 fl. oz. olive oil;
2 lb. skinned tomatoes with pips and cores removed;
salt and pepper to season;
3 large, fresh basil leaves

(removed for service) or 1 rounded teaspoon crumbled, dried basil;
1 given quantity *Tagliatelle Verdi* (p. 28);
Salsa Pizzaiola (p. 85).

Method: Heat oil until sizzling merrily, add tomato flesh and chosen type of basil and simmer gently until tender. Season to taste with salt and pepper and remove leaves if using fresh basil. Meanwhile, place green noodles in a very roomy pan liberally filled with fast-boiling, slightly salted water. Cook for 11½/12 minutes. Strain, turn into chosen serving dish and pour tomato sauce on top.

Note: If preferred, you may use ordinary *Tagliatelle* which is also ribbon noodles but creamy yellow in colour and if preferred you can likewise *purée* the sauce before pouring overall and hand grated *Parmesan* cheese separately.

CANNELLONI CON SALSA SPINACI
(Tube Pasta – Spinach Sauce)

Ingredients:

Up to 9 bought *Cannelloni* or for home-made the number of squares available from the given quantity of home-made pasta;

a little butter;

about 4 oz. grated *Parmesan* cheese;

6 fl. oz. strongly reduced chicken or meat stock;

Salsa Spinaci (p. 84).

Method: Slip *Cannelloni* into plenty of slightly salted fast boiling water in a roomy pan and allow to bubble steadily for 5 minutes. Lift them out very carefully on a slice, open out, spread on a cold surface and when completely cold spread each one with its chosen stuffing. Then roll them up as you would pancakes and arrange a layer of them on the base of a generously buttered heat-resistant dish. Dot with flakes of butter, cover with a generous layer of *Parmesan* and pour stock overall. Cover with lid or piece of kitchen foil, place in the oven one shelf above centre and bake at Gas Mark 4 for 10 minutes for 1 layer, 12–13 minutes for 2 layers and 14–16 minutes for 3 layers. If liked extra cheese may be handed separately with a small jug of additional, melted butter.

TORTA DI PASTA SPINACI (Spaghetti Pie)

Ingredients:

1 tin concentrated tomato soup or ½ pint *Salsa di Pomidoro* (p. 82);

1½ lb. raw minced beef, lamb or veal;

1 level teaspoon pepper;

1 level dessertspoon powdered sage;

1 small tin spinach *purée* or ½ lb. fresh cooked (p. 68);

1 teacup strongly-reduced stock;

¾ lb. spaghetti;

3¾ pints cold water;

2 oz. butter or 2½ fl. oz. olive oil;

4 oz. grated *Parmesan* cheese;

1 level teaspoon salt;

freshly milled black peppercorns to taste.

Method: Cook spaghetti in fast-boiling salted water for 9 minutes. Drain. Rub a large (10″ × 6″) pie dish with ½ the butter or oil. Cover base with a layer of cooked spaghetti. Mix together in a bowl the soup or *Salsa,* meat, pepper, sage, stock and liquor from the tin of spinach. Place the layer of mixture over spaghetti, dab with ½ spinach, sprinkle with ½ the cheese, repeat using remaining spaghetti, meat mixture and spinach. Sprinkle with remaining cheese, dot with flakes of remaining butter. Refrigerate until needed. Just before service, bake for 30 minutes, Gas Mark 6, and serve piping hot.

VERMICELLI CON FUNGHI (with Mushrooms)

Ingredients:

¾ lb. *Vermicelli;*

¼ lb. mushrooms and/or their stalks;

1 rounded teaspoon freshly milled marjoram;

2 rounded tablespoons freshly milled parsley heads;

salt and black pepper to season;

2 fl. oz. olive oil.

Method: As *Vermicelli* is the thinnest of all the pastas and the only similar item which is even more slender is Rice *Vermicelli,* strictly speaking it needs only 8 minutes in fast-boiling, slightly salted water. In a separate pan heat oil, slice mushrooms and their stalks very finely and when oil is hot toss in mushrooms and shake over heat for not more than 4 minutes. Turn fast over well strained *Vermicelli,* turn in all remaining ingredients. Taste, correct seasoning with salt and pepper and serve with pork spare ribs.

RISO
(Rice)

THE RICE YOU CHOOSE

Wild Rice: The most luxurious of all is in the price bracket of truffles, *foie gras* and caviare.

Vermicelli Rice: Chinese – best fried.

Risotta: Italian – self-explanatory.

Patna Rice: Not hard grained; scarcely at all transparent; white and cylindrical. For general use.

Glutinous Rice: Chinese – much used instead of flour, egg and bread-crumbs for coating meat balls, etc.

Brown Rice: Long grained; much venerated against white rice for its nutritive qualities.

Basmati Rice: 'Indian' – ideal for Curries.

Arborio Rice: Yellow rice with a nutty flavour; excellent for Paellas, Pilaffs and Curries. Has special virtue of being a non-sticky rice.

HOW TO PRESERVE RICE

This is an old storage method given to us many years ago by a friend from Pakistan.

Ingredients:

4 lb. rice;

5 fl. oz. crude or refined castor oil;

$\frac{1}{4}$ lb. whole, small, dried, red chillies.

Method: Place the rice in a huge open container, add the oil and work through well-washed fingers until it is evenly distributed throughout the rice. Store in a lidded stone jar with the chillies distributed throughout. **Do not** use this rice before it is at least 1 year old.

Note: All the above was done by us under our friend's watchful eye. When a year later we cooked our first batch, we discovered for ourselves that the difference between ordinary shop rice and 'vintage rice' is most impressive. Now we 'put down' for our storage area or 'go down' a regular rotation of supplies every 3 months and all containers are carefully date-lined.

BASIC SWEATED RICE

Ingredients:

½ lb. chosen rice (for super extravagance Wild rice, otherwise use *Patna, Arborio,* Brown or *Risotto* types);

1 chopped shallot or small onion;

2 oz. butter;

1 quart chosen liquor.

Method: Melt butter in shallow pan. Chop onion or shallot finely, add to hot melted butter, add rice and with, ideally, a perforated metal spoon, turn over moderate heat until the rice is faintly coloured, i.e. 4 minutes. Turn into a casserole pot, cover with all chosen liquor, then with lid and place in oven, 1 shelf above centre, at Gas Mark 7, for approximately 20 minutes, by which time rice will be cooked without being pappy and will have absorbed all the liquor.

Addenda to this Basic: We said **liquor.** It can begin at the bottom by being 1 quart water, rise to being 1 quart ordinary bone stock or any special stock: meat, game, poultry or fish. It can then rise again with 4 fl. oz. of dry white wine or of red cooking wine. Thus you deduct the 4 fl. oz. from the 40 fl. oz. which comprise 1 quart and put only 36 fl. oz. of chosen stock in addition to the chosen wine. Finally on the highest rung of the ladder, you use this basic method with wild rice, 33 fl. oz. stock, 5 fl. oz. dry sherry or Madeira and 2 fl. oz. cooking brandy.

BASIC FRIED RICE

This is identical to Sweated Rice, except that when the first frying stage has been completed you add 1 quart of chosen liquor very gradually in small doses and allow the grains to absorb each addition as it swells in the frying pan, over moderate heat, until the whole amount has been absorbed in this manner. Stir throughout cooking.

BASIC PAR-BOILED, OVEN-FINISHED RICE

Ingredients:

½ lb. *Patna* rice;

1 oz. butter;

1 oz. oil;

1 pint strained stock from which the fatty top has not been removed.

Method: Toss the rice into plenty of fast-boiling, slightly salted water as for Basic Boiled Rice, but cook only for 6 minutes. Then strain, turn into a smallish, lidded casserole, cover with stock and cook gently in oven, Gas Mark 5, 1 shelf above centre until all liquor is absorbed. Work in oil and butter very thoroughly and serve with any kebab meats on skewers.

BASIC GRAIN-SEPARATE BOILED RICE

Ingredients:

½ lb. *Patna* rice or brown (health) rice;

1 rounded dessertspoon cooking salt;

4½ pints water.

Method: Bring water and salt to hard rolling boil. Slide in the rice, stir until boiling resumes and reduce heat a little thereafter, so that you achieve a steady, rolling, small-bubbled boil. Maintain for exactly 11½ minutes. It must be slightly *al dente*, i.e. firm to the teeth, not a despondent, collapsed grain pap. Turn off heat, stir once with wooden spoon, pour immediately through sieve, shake off surplus water and you will find that your rice is absolutely grain separate.

For a more distinguished presentation of boiled rice, you turn strained rice into a bowl, add butter or oil and mix with a fork.

RISOTTO DI FUNGHI (Rice and Mushrooms)

Ingredients:

1½ oz. butter or 1½ fl. oz. olive oil;

1 shallot or small onion, very thinly sliced;

6 oz. thinly sliced mushrooms;

6 fl. oz. dry white cooking wine

and 27 fl. oz. boiling stock or 33 fl. oz. boiling stock;

1½ oz. *Parmesan* or other hard cheese;

12 oz. *Arborio* or *Risotto* rice.

Method: Heat butter or oil in a large, heavy pan and *sauté* the onion over a low heat until soft and transparent but not brown. Add mushrooms and stir well. Pour in the wine or 6 fl. oz. stock and continue cooking until almost completely evaporated. Add rice and continue cooking until this begins to change colour, then add 4 fl. oz. stock. Cook until the stock has been absorbed by the rice, then add another 4 fl. oz. stock and continue in this manner until all the stock has been absorbed. This process will take about 25/30 minutes, and by the end the rice will be perfectly tender, with each grain separate. Add the cheese, stir well, cover the pan and leave the *Risotto* to settle for 2–3 minutes before serving. Serve with a bowl of additional grated *Parmesan* cheese.

RISI E BISI VENEZIANA

Ingredients:

½ lb. *Patna* rice;

1 quart good bone stock;

2 rashers de-rinded, diced, streaky bacon;

1 small onion or shallot diced small;

1 oz. olive oil or butter;

6 oz. cooked, fresh peas;

salt and pepper to season.

Method: Dissolve the butter or heat oil in a small frying-pan. When sizzling, fry onion or shallot for 1 minute, turn in rice, turn over until well-impregnated with the butter or oil and slightly yellowed. Turn into a lidded casserole, cover with stock and lid. Cook in oven, middle shelf Gas Mark 5, for 1 hour 10 minutes, by which time rice will have taken up almost all the liquor and will be cooked and grain-separate. Meanwhile, fry the bacon dry over very moderate heat until cooked. Add bacon and fatty juices to cooked rice. Also add hot peas, turn thoroughly and correct seasoning as desired with salt and pepper.

For the Liver Version

Use 2 oz. butter and 1 oz. olive oil and 4 oz. calves' liver diced small. When butter sizzles fry liver gently until cooked but **not** over-cooked.

For the Baby Marrow (Zucchini) Version

Top, tail and dice 2 baby marrows. Steam over hot water or soft-fry slowly in 1 oz. butter and 1 oz. oil. Stir into basic *Risi e Bisi* mixture, after cooking.

For the Shrimp Version

Add to basic *Risi e Bisi* mixture 4 oz. shelled shrimps heated in ½ oz. of oil on floor of oven under a scrap of foil.

Please remember all these variations are added **when rice is cooked.**

RISOTTO ALLA MILANESE. No. 1

(Milanese Rice)

Ingredients:

12 oz. *Risotto* rice;

1 quart of chicken stock (substitute any white meat bone stock);

1 pkt. saffron pistils;*

2 oz. grated *Parmesan* cheese and a small bowlful to hand

separately;

2 oz. butter and a little jug of melted butter to hand separately;

1 shallot or very small onion chopped finely;

salt and pepper to season.

Method: Dissolve 1 oz. butter in a thick frying pan. Add the onion or shallot and stir, then fry on over low heat until onion is half tender, approximately 4/5 minutes. Add rice and saffron, turn well to impregnate rice, then add first smallish teacupful of stock. Stir again and giving only an occasional stir hereafter, allow rice to absorb this liquor. Add another cupful of stock and so continue until all stock has been absorbed and rice is cooked but not pappy! Stir in remaining 1 oz. butter and the 2 oz. cheese. Taste, correct seasoning with salt and white pepper.

*Saffron is the dried, or powdered, dried pistils of the autumn crocus *Crocus Sativus*.

Note: From now onwards through all *Risotto* variants the method remains constant and only the ingredients and quantities vary.

RISOTTO BIANCO (White Rice)

Follow the instructions for *Risotto Milanese*. Use 12 oz. *Risotto* rice to 1½ pints water and ½ pint white wine (or use all water), 2 oz. butter, 1 shallot or very small onion chopped finely.

RISOTTO ALLA MILANESE. No. 2 (for Fish)

If wishing to make a *Risotto* for use with fish, follow the instructions for *Risotto Milanese No. 1* (above) with 12 oz. *Risotto* rice, 1¾ pints fish stock (p. 42), ¼ pint dry white wine, salt and pepper to season, 1 shallot or small onion and 1 oz. butter for frying rice.

RISOTTO ALLA VERONESE

(Veronese Rice with Ham)

Follow the instructions for *Risotto Bianco*. When completed stir in 3 oz. fine dice of lean ham and season with white pepper.

RISO ALLA FONDUTA (Rice with *Fonduta*)

Is plain boiled rice (p. 37), thoroughly drained, and served with *Fonduta* (p. 80).

RISO AL LIMONE E FORMAGGIO
(Lemon Rice with Cheese)

Ingredients:

¾ lb. boiled rice (p. 37);
strained juice of 1 medium lemon;
3 oz. grated *Parmesan* cheese;

white pepper;
3 eggs;
2 oz. butter.

Method: When rice is cooked and thoroughly drained, dissolve butter in a roomy pan, turn in rice over low heat and turn until thoroughly impregnated. Draw pan to side of heat. Beat eggs thoroughly. Beat in cheese and lemon juice. Add a good flavouring of pepper and return rice in pan over gentle heat. Then with a wooden spoon, stir in egg/cheese mixture, turning and stirring as you pour in mixture in a thin stream. When rice becomes creamy, eggs have self-sauced themselves and cheese is melted, serve at once, and on no account allow mixture to boil or eggs will become nasty little gritty bits!

PESCE

(Fish)

SOGLIOLE ALLA VENEZIANA (Sole or Plaice)

There are 2 ways of making this famous Italian dish, with sole or with plaice, using whole fish of suitable size for serving as 1 portion per fish.

Ingredients:

1 sole on the bone weighing 12–14 oz.;

1 oz. butter;

1 dessertspoon finely chopped fresh mint leaves;

1 teaspoon freshly milled fresh parsley heads;

¼ small, peeled, crushed garlic clove;

salt and pepper;

1 small shallot or onion;

3 fl. oz. water;

3 fl. oz. inexpensive Italian white cooking wine.

Method: Skin the sole (or see that fishmonger does so for you) and then run the tip of a knife down each side of the upper part to open out 2 'lips' on either side of the bone. Pare these back and if you wish to be an absolute perfectionist ease out the spine bone. Now prepare the stuffing. Work ½ the butter with the parsley, mint, garlic and a light seasoning of salt and pepper to form a paste. Divide this and insert in the 2 fillet 'lips'. Press down and prepare the sauce. Dissolve the remaining butter in a small pan, fry the finely chopped shallot or onion very gently until tender but not browned. Stir in the wine and simmer on for 10 minutes. Add the water, correct the seasoning with salt and pepper and allow to continue simmering while you grill the sole. To do this, place a piece of buttered paper over the stuffed upper part and grill the under part first. Turn over, remove paper and grill the upper part, brushing this with a little extra butter before so doing. When cooked, lift onto a heated plate and pour the sauce over all.

Note: This recipe goes back to the Renaissance when Venice was the great gastronomic 'Mecca' of Europe.

SOGLIOLE ALLA PARMIGIANA
(Sole with Cheese)

Ingredients for 1 serving:

one 12–14 oz. sole;

1 oz. butter;

1 fl. oz. fish stock;

salt;

black pepper;

1 oz. grated *Parmesan* cheese.

Method: Rub the interior of a heat-resistant, shallow dish with butter. Skin sole on both sides removing head and tail. Cover with lid or aluminium kitchen foil and cook middle shelf Gas Mark 4 for 20 minutes (only 12 minutes if oven is preheated and already hot); scatter *Parmesan* over fish, add fish stock and season with salt and pepper. Cook on with light foil covering, for a further 5 minutes. Serve from container.

SOGLIOLE AL MARSALA
(Sole or Plaice with Marsala)

Ingredients:

9 oz. sole fillets (4);

the bones, fish head and tail for fish stock with 1 leaf lemon peel;

2 parsley stalks;

2/3 peppercorns and 1 very small (optional) sprig of fennel leaf;

flour for dusting fillets;

1 oz. butter;

2 tablespoons *Marsala;*

2 tablespoons fish stock;

2 tablespoons thick cream (whipping or double);

salt and black pepper to season.

Method: Pass fillets through flour and dust off surplus. Dissolve butter in small frying pan. When this 'sings', slide in fillets, season with salt and pepper and allow to cook over moderate heat until they contract and become firm; but for no longer than this please as further cooking merely toughens. Remove fillets, drain and keep warm while making sauce. Add all remaining ingredients to pan residue, stir and allow to bubble fiercely to a coating sauce consistency (2–3 minutes maximum). Pour sauce through strainer over fillets and, optionally, garnish with lemon slices.

The Fish Stock

Place sole or plaice, head, tail, bones and skins in a pan. Cover with cold water. Add fennel, parsley stalks, peppercorns, lemon peel, raise to a steady simmer. Maintain for exactly 20 minutes. Strain, return resultant liquor to a small pan, simmer down to $\frac{1}{8}$ its bulk, then use as required. Surplus fish stock can be refrigerated for 24 hours at least.

RISOTTO DI SCAMPI

(Rice with Scampi or Dublin Bay Prawns)

Ingredients:

2 oz. finely chopped shallots or onion;

2 fl. oz. olive oil;

6 oz. risotto rice;

1 pint shelled prawns;

1¼ pints fish stock (see *Sogliole al Marsala* p. 42);

¼ pint dry white Italian wine;

black pepper to season and a very little salt;

2 pkts. saffron (standard).

Method: Heat oil until it 'sings' in frying pan. Slide in finely chopped, peeled onions or shallots and fry over very low heat until nearly tender but not browned. Add rice and saffron, stir with wooden spoon and stir turn until rice grains become very yellow and oil-infused. Add white wine. Stir and continue stirring until rice has swollen sufficiently to take up this quantity of fluid. Add ¼ of stock, and repeat 3 times more until all stock is absorbed. Almost immediately after last addition add raw, shelled, chopped scampi or prawns. Stir in, cook, with careful stir turning until rice and fish are cooked. Season with salt and pepper. Optionally ½ pint young, cooked peas may also be stirred in just before completion and grated *Parmesan* cheese may be handed separately.

SCAMPI ALLA GRIGLIA

(Scampi or Dublin Bay Prawns)

Ingredients:

8 raw scampi or Dublin Bay prawns;

½ lb. rice;

1 pkt. saffron;

2 oz. pine kernels;

4 oz. shelled, cooked peas;

salt and pepper;

(optional) 3 fl. oz. cooking brandy if wishing to 'flame' for service;

(optional) crushed garlic clove;

4 large fresh basil leaves;

olive oil.

Method: Take 2 long slim skewers, push point of each through scampi. To do this really successfully hold unshelled scampi tail to headless end and drive skewer tip through centre of both sides thus imposing on them a very simple form of spatchcocking. Brush liberally with olive oil. Scatter with ½ chopped basil (or substitute parsley), drip more olive oil over each skewer load when laid out on grill rack of grill pan. Slide under heated grill at low position and allow to cook for 2–3 minutes on first side. Remove, turn over, re-brush with oil, sprinkle with remaining basil or parsley, return to same cooking position and grill on for 1 minute, then bash down with a heavy piece of wood or meat batter to flatten and to split shells a little. Finish grilling as before for a further $1\frac{1}{2}$ to 2 minutes. Place on heat-resistant dish. Pour brandy overall and flame it.

TRIGLIE ALLA GRIGLIA
(Grilled Red Mullet with Fennel)

Ingredients:

medium red mullet;

a little olive oil;

a generous pinch to each fish of

very finely chopped leaf of fennel;

salt and pepper.

Method: Make sure mullet are well cleaned and keep a sharp eye on the fishmonger (or yourself) to ensure livers are left inside. Season interiors lightly with salt and pepper. Brush all over exteriors with olive oil. Score deeply, making 3 criss-crossed cuts over each. Rub in the fennel and grill under medium grill. Serve with plain melted butter in a separate container and also lemon slices (optional).

TRIGLIE ALLA VENEZIANA (Red Mullet)

Ingredients:

4 small, cleaned red mullet with heads left on;

4 fresh mint leaves;

4 small pinches of pulverised garlic;

a little sifted flour;

2/3 fl. oz. olive oil;

2 oz. finely chopped, peeled onion;

5 fl. oz. inexpensive cooking-type Italian white wine;

1 tablespoon white wine vinegar;

salt and pepper to season;

1 small, thin-skinned orange, peeled and with pith removed, then cut into skin-less segments.

Method: Stuff each cleaned fish with 1 mint leaf and a pinch of garlic, turn fish thoroughly in flour, dust off surplus and heat olive oil in shallow pan. Fry fish over moderate heat on both sides, lift out, drain and set on a heated dish. Fry the onion in oil residue until soft but not browned. Work in wine and wine vinegar and simmer gently for long enough to reduce total fluid content to a mere $2\frac{1}{2}$ fl. oz. Sprinkle the fish lightly with salt and pepper. Sieve sauce over fish and arrange a few orange segments over each one. Serve either hot or cold.

Note: For those who, like ourselves, detest mint, fennel, fish's own herb, may be substituted with excellent but NOT classic results.

COZZE AL VINO BIANCO (Baked Mussels)

Ingredients:

6 pints scrubbed, bearded mussels;

7½ fl. oz. inexpensive dry white wine;

1 very finely chopped shallot or onion;

1 teacup finely grated, soft brown breadcrumbs;

3 rounded tablespoons finely chopped parsley;

3 oz. finely grated *Parmesan* cheese;

pepper to season.

Method: When mussels are clean, set in a steamer over fast-boiling water. Steam for a minimum 1 minute, maximum 1½ and discard any mussels which have not opened by this time. Remove empty half-shells as soon as mussels are cool and arrange mussels on half-shells over base of shallow heat-resistant container suitable for table service. Sprinkle breadcrumbs all over mussels. Then sprinkle parsley, then cheese, then onion and finally flick wine over all, so that the dry ingredients become thoroughly moistened with it. Season with generous gratings of freshly milled black peppercorns. Tent lightly in kitchen foil. Bake at Gas Mark 6, 1 shelf above centre, for 15 minutes. Serve with plenty of brown bread and butter, preferably hot. This is as you know only a matter of wrapping brown rolls or a small brown loaf loosely in kitchen foil and heating through – 7/8 minutes for the rolls, 10/12 for the loaf at Gas Mark 3, 1 shelf above centre.

FRITTO MISTO MARE (Fried Fish miscellany)

Ingredients:

small pieces of octopus tentacles;

shelled prawns;

whitebait (as a substitute for Mediterranean or Adriatic minute fish of many varieties);

baby red mullet (when possible);

baby octopus quartered;

scollops (unorthodox);

little pieces of sole or plaice fillet;

flour;

hot oil;

lemon;

salt and pepper.

Method: Only the cheaper restaurants immerse everything in batter, you and we merely dip the neat pieces of each item in flour, pat this well in, dust off surplus and fry in hot oil in a deep fryer. Drain on absorbent kitchen paper, pile on a heated d'oyley covered dish and season lightly with salt and pepper. Border with fat pieces of de-pipped lemon. These are especially good when accompanied by a sauceboat of Green Mayonnaise (p. 86).

SARDE RIPIENE (Stuffed, Fresh Sardines)

Ingredients:

2 lb. fresh sardines;

6 oz. fine, soft breadcrumbs;

4 oz. grated *Parmesan* cheese;

1 large egg;

2 fat tablespoons fresh, milled parsley heads;

1 scant flat teaspoon salt;

1 scant flat saltspoon of black pepper;

strained juice of ½ medium lemon;

2 fl. oz. olive oil;

2/3 oz. fish stock (p. 42) (see *Sogliole al Marsala*).

Method: Top, tail, split (head to tail down centre of belly), clean wash and wipe sardines. Remove spine and all small bones. Make up stuffing by mixing breadcrumbs, cheese, salt, pepper and parsley together until well blended. Bind with beaten egg and if too stiff moisten with a few extra drops of fish stock. Spread stuffing down the centre of each fish. Roll each one up. Heat olive oil in frying pan. When this 'sings' lay in the rolled boneless sardine 'parcels' side by side. Fry fairly briskly on both sides until just browned – rather fast. Add stock, reduce heat to low, cover with lid or aluminium foil and simmer on for 8/10 minutes. Lift onto heated serving dish, bubble up pan residue, stir well, pour overall and moisten the dishful with the lemon juice and a further light sprinkling of salt and pepper. Optionally scatter fish, chopped or milled parsley overall.

ANGUILLE ALLA FIORENTINA (Eels)

Ingredients:

2 lb. fresh skinned eel cut into 2″ lengths;

2 crushed garlic cloves;

2 torn bayleaves;

salt and pepper to season;

2 fl. oz. olive oil;

2 fl. oz. fish stock (see *Sogliole al Marsala* p. 42);

1 level teacup of fine soft breadcrumbs.

Method: Brush base and sides of medium pie dish with a little extra olive oil. Pass raw, skinned, eel pieces through breadcrumbs in shallow container, pat well in and lay ½ over oiled base. Work given oil with garlic. Flick ⅓ over crumbed eel in pie dish. Tear 1 bay leaf in 2 and lay over. Repeat with remaining eels and second bay leaf. Add remaining crumbs. Flick with remaining oil/garlic mixture. Season stock fairly strongly with salt and pepper. Drip evenly overall. Place in oven 1 shelf below centre at Gas Mark 3 and bake until eels are tender and crumb topping is richly browned, approximately 40/50 minutes depending on thickness of eel pieces.

BACCALA ALLA VENEZIANA (Dried, Salt Cod)

The salted cod sold in Britain is not exactly the same as the one used along the Adriatic for this famous Venetian dish but it is very good and by no means to be scorned.

Ingredients:

1½ lb. dried salt cod;

3 medium shallots or small onions;

4–5 anchovy fillets (from oil not brine);

1 oz. butter;

3 fl. oz. olive oil;

1 pint *Béchamel* Sauce;

pepper to season.

Method: Cut cod into 1″ wide, 2–2½″ long rectangles. Place in a roomy container, cover liberally with cold water and soak for a minimum 14 hours. Drain, wipe and set near cooker. Dissolve butter with 1 fl. oz. olive oil, when this 'sings', fry peeled, chopped onions or shallots until well-coloured and partially softened for 5 minutes over gentle heat. Add fish and, still over very gentle heat, turn until thoroughly oil-impregnated, cover and cook on, giving occasional shakes to pan, for 15 minutes. Drain onions or shallots and fish pieces and set in a heat-resistant dish. Chop anchovy fillets small, stir into *Béchamel,* pour sauce over fish. Cover with lid or aluminium foil, place in oven 1 shelf below centre at Gas Mark 2 to cook gently until tender. Approximately 1 hour. Serve from container.

The Béchamel

1½ oz. butter, 1½ oz. sifted flour, 1 pint milk, pepper to season. Dissolve butter in small thick pan. Stir in flour and work with wooden spoon until *roux* (which it has become) forms a thick paste which leaves sides on base of pan and forms a soft ball. Dilute with about ¼ of milk, ease *roux* off pan base with wooden spoon then leave until milk begins to boil. Stir quite slowly, gradually increasing speed. Finally beat hard until absolutely smooth. Repeat this 3 times more with remaining milk. If considered too thick, dilute with a little more milk but this is purely a matter of choice.

POLLO IN PEPERONATA
(Chicken in Pimento Sauce)

Ingredients:

1 given batch sieved *Peperonata* (p. 87);

1 small chicken;

8 oz. shell pasta;

optional side dishes of grated

Parmesan cheese and Mango chutney;

1 oz. butter;

salt and pepper to season.

Method: Place chicken in a meat baking tin, season with salt and pepper, rub upper parts with butter, cover breast bone lightly with a small piece of foil and bake Gas Mark 5, 1 shelf above centre, until juice runs faintly pink when fattest thigh is prodded with skewer or tip of pointed knife (approximately 45 minutes). As soon as chicken is just cool enough to handle, rip off skin (optional) and divide into neat portions (essential). Pile onto a heated dish, rub sauce overall through a sieve and border with the shell pasta, which has already been tossed into fast boiling, salted water and simmered for 12 minutes or serve with grain-separate boiled rice (p. 37).

POLLO GRAZIELLE (Chicken with Wine and Cream)

A very delicate dish.

Ingredients:

one 3¾ lb. roasting chicken;

gros sel or Malden sea salt and freshly milled black peppercorns;

4 oz. chicken fat;

10 small, peeled, whole shallots;

6 oz. slim, young carrots, sliced in fairly thin rounds;

1 *bouquet garni* (herb faggot);

¼ pint dry white wine;

¼ pint double or whipping cream.

Method: Remove wing tips and parson's nose from chicken and set aside. Remove interior fat. Rub chicken all over with *gros sel* or Malden sea salt and pepper. Dissolve 4 oz. chicken fat in small pan, press through a sieve and use ½ of it to brush over the bird. Place bird in casserole over prepared bed of shallots, carrots and *bouquet garni*. Pour remaining chicken fat overall. Cover with lid and cook on middle shelf of oven at Gas Mark 4 for 35 minutes. Remove skin and cut bird into standard portions, i.e. the halved breasts or *suprêmes,* the halved legs and thighs and the skinned wings with tips chopped off. Keep warm. Smash down the carcase (an excellent use to which you can put a silly rolling pin with handles on the ends!), place in second lidded casserole with the raw wing tips, parson's nose, unskinned neck, the split-cleaned gizzard and the heart. Cover liberally with water or stock, cover with lid and cook in the oven, bottom shelf, Gas Mark 2, for 4 hours. Strain stock, pour ½ over pan residue in chicken casserole and simmer until completely tender. Sieve and return to pot with the wine. Reduce to 1 pint 7½ fl. oz. Add the cream and reduce for the last time to 1 pint of syrupy liquor. Taste, correct seasoning with salt and pepper and immerse chicken portions in sauce for 1 minute to impregnate. Arrange on dish and pour sauce overall.

BUDINO DI POLLO

(Chicken Mousse with Chicken Liquor)

This is a most unusual recipe, simple to make and very delicate.

Ingredients:

2¼ pints of very strongly reduced, well seasoned chicken stock;

3 oz. finely grated *Parmesan* cheese;

salt and pepper to season and 1 generous pinch of nutmeg;

4½ oz. raw chicken flesh;

3 eggs.

Method: Mince the raw chicken and then pound in a mortar with a pestle (or emulsify or liquidise) adding 1 or 2 teaspoons of the chicken stock as you work. When mixture is smooth and creamy rub through a sieve.

Season, add the cheese and nutmeg and beaten eggs. Divide the mixture between 4 ramequins or little individual soufflé moulds; these must first be rubbed carefully with butter inside. Cover with little 'lids' of aluminium foil. Sink into a shallow pan containing just enough boiling water to come only half-way up the chosen containers. Poach extremely gently over a low heat until just set, which should take no more than 12 minutes or the resultant little moulds will get too dry. As soon as they can be turned out, slip them onto the centre base of heated soup bowls. Pour the boiling stock on top and serve immediately.

POLLO ALLA DIAVOLA DI FIRENZE
(Spatchcocked, Devilled, Grilled Chicken)

This is a most interesting and highly spiced version of Spatchcocked chicken. So first we will explain the method of spatchcocking for a $3\frac{1}{4}$–$3\frac{1}{2}$ lb. roasting bird as baby chickens for individual servings are both far more costly and far more difficult to find anyway!

You will need 2 long slim metal skewers (10″) and a sharp strong knife. Leave the skin on the bird. Cut from the tip of the breastbone right through and down to the end of the wishbone. Sever the skin on the leg/thigh pieces around where the thigh attaches each one to the main carcase. Flatten out the bird and then bring the 2 (loosened) leg pieces up until the bone tips touch at centre. Skewer through the flesh right across to hold them together, rather like up-raised clasped hands! Then sever the joining skin of the wings and bring them round to centre in the same way at the opposite end. This enables you to give one or two smart smacks over the carcase with a classic meat-batter or (a cleaned) old-fashioned flatiron and thus you ensure all flesh is exposed to even grill heat.

Now make up the spreading mixture:

Assemble: $1\frac{1}{2}$ oz. peeled, chopped onion, 2 rounded tablespoons parsley, milled or chopped with the small head-stalks left on, a $\frac{1}{2}″$ piece of root ginger, 1 peeled garlic clove, $3\frac{1}{2}$ fl. oz. olive oil, 1 flat teaspoon salt, 1 flat eggspoon freshly milled black peppercorns, 2 basil leaves (when possible). Put all into a mortar and pound down to a paste with a pestle (or emulsify). Spread spatchcocked chicken on skin-side with $\frac{1}{2}$ this mixture. Place on a piece of oiled aluminium foil on the base of a grill. Ignore the existence of the grill pan or rack, adjust grill heat to half strength. Allow chicken to turn a good rich golden brown on this side. It should take a maximum of 25 minutes for given weight, turning it round (not over) so that outstretched chicken is evenly cooked. Then spread remaining paste over reverse side and repeat grilling this side for a further maximum 25 minutes. Serve with a tossed, dressed, green or mixed salad.

POLLO ALLA PADOVANA

(Chicken with Lemon Sauce)

Ingredients:

one 3½–4 lb. roasting chicken;

12 oz. finely chopped, peeled onions;

1 oz. butter;

1 fl. oz. oil;

the strained juice of ½ a large lemon;

1 separated egg yolk;

salt and black pepper to season.

Method: Dissolve butter and heat through with oil in a roomy frying pan, add the prepared onions and fry gently until soft but not browned. Skin the chicken, cut into neat pieces, 2 wings, 2 legs, 4 breast pieces, 2 thighs, 1 parson's nose, 1 wishbone, 2 'oysters'. Add chicken pieces to pan contents. Season with salt and pepper; when well-impregnated turn all into a lidded casserole and cook in the oven at Gas Mark 4 one shelf above centre for 1 hour. Work egg yolk and lemon juice together, stir into piping hot casserole contents until smoothly blended but on no account allow to boil again or egg might curdle! This is both unusual and very popular.

POLLO ALL' ARETINA (Chicken with Peas and Rice)

Ingredients:

one 3 lb. roasting chicken;

9 oz. (peeled weight) onions;

¾ pint stock from chicken carcase (well smashed down please);

1 gill dry Italian white wine;

¾ pint shelled, fresh peas;

6 oz. *Risotto* rice;

3 oz. olive oil;

salt and black pepper to season;

2 sprigs thyme;

1 'leaf' of very thinly-cut lemon peel.

Method: Chop peeled onions. Heat oil in frying pan and when hot fry onion dice gently until tender but not browned. Divide chicken into neat portions and add to onions after first 5 minutes. Season with salt and pepper. Fish out chicken pieces after a further 5 minutes. Place in a casserole. Add to pan residue, wine, rice, thyme and lemon peel. Now keep turning to stop rice sticking, for a further 5 minutes. Empty over chicken pieces in casserole. Cover with a lid. Cook 1 shelf below centre for 1 hour Gas Mark 4, by which time rice will have absorbed almost all liquor and chicken will be tender and deliciously infused with flavours.

PETTI DI POLLO PARMIGIANI

(Chicken Breasts with Ham and Cheese)

This is a particularly delicious, easy way of giving a delicate treatment to chickens' breasts. Moreover if you care to remove and divide the thigh and leg pieces, skin and cut out the bones so that the pieces may be used flat, there is nothing to stop you using these sections of the birds as well. They are just not the classic Italian *Petti di Pollo!*

Ingredients:

To 2 skinned breasts of chicken assemble:

2 oz. finely grated *Parmesan* cheese;

2 large slices of cooked ham;

pepper to season;

2 oz. butter;

2 fl. oz. olive oil;

4 oz. mushrooms and their stalks.

Note: We deliberately omit the classic white truffles of Bologna!

Method: Pare away the chicken breasts and bat them out a little with a meat batter dipped into cold water. (This stops the batting from breaking down the surface of the flesh and rendering it unsightly.) Dissolve and heat butter and oil in a small pan, pour into a shallow fireproof dish. Cut right through the 2 breasts **across** their entire length to make 4 thinner portions of the original size. Pass through the oil/butter mixture, then allow them to sink down into it and cover with either a lid or aluminium kitchen foil. Cook at Gas Mark 4, middle shelf, for a maximum 25 minutes. Season with pepper. Lay halved slices of the ham on top of each. Slice scalded, unskinned mushrooms and their stalks, finely turning into hot pan-residue. Fry over low heat until collapsed (2–3 minutes). Arrange around chicken pieces, sprinkle on given cheese, moisten overall with 1 or 2 teaspoons of pan's oil/butter mixture and return under lid or other covering to oven at same temperature but 1 shelf **above** centre, for 5 minutes or until cheese is nicely melted over each. Lift all out on to a heated dish. Serve with *Crocchette di Spinaci* (p. 70).

ANITRA ALL'OLIO (Duck with Olives)

Ingredients:

1 young duck;

2 duck livers;

2 gizzards;

2 hearts;

2 necks;

6 oz. onions (peeled weight);

1 rounded tablespoon flour;

24 large green olives;

salt and pepper;

1¼ pints strongly reduced duck stock;

8 fl. oz. red *Chianti;*

2 fl. oz. olive oil.

Method: Remove the leg thigh pieces and divide the parson's nose, the wings, the wishbone section and the 2 breasts, halving these last. Smash down the carcase to a crushed ruin. Place in a roomy pan; add gizzards and necks. Cover liberally with cold water. Bring to the boil, skim, refresh with an additional glass of cold water, re-boil and level off at a steady simmer. Maintain for 1½ hours. Strain, return liquor to cleaned pan and simmer down until reduced to given 1¼ pints. Slice onions very thinly, chop and heat oil in a frying pan. Fry until soft but not browned. Press into a sieve, return oil residue to pan, set onions aside. Fry duck pieces in hot oil until browned over a fairly strong heat. Place these in a casserole and work flour down to a paste in pan residue. Dilute gradually with *Chianti* stirring until smooth between each addition. Repeat with stock. Peel all olives from stones, chop half of them finely. Work into sauce in pan. Then work in finely chopped livers and hearts and simmer very gently for 10 minutes more. Pour all over duck in casserole. Cover and cook under lid, Gas Mark 4, middle shelf for 1½ hours or until tender. Slice in remaining olives and serve from casserole.

CONIGLIO IN AGRODOLCE

(Sicilian Rabbit in Sweet/Sour Sauce)

Ingredients:

1 young rabbit, skinned, drawn and divided into the following pieces:—

4 legs, 1 head, 1 liver, 2 kidneys and body cut into 4 pieces;

seasoned flour;

2 oz. raw, unsalted pork fat in fine dice;

½ pint wine vinegar;

1 gill tomato pulp (skinned, cored and de-seeded);

3 outer sticks white celery;

12 small stoned or peeled, chopped, green olives;

1 rounded tablespoon pressed capers;

3 flat tablespoons castor sugar;

1 mean flat teaspoon salt;

1 scant flat eggspoon black pepper.

Method: Turn rabbit pieces thoroughly in seasoned flour. Put fat dice in frying pan over very low heat and allow fat to run and dice to shrivel. Step up heat to brisk, fry prepared rabbit pieces until browned all over. Lift into a casserole. Sprinkle in olives, finely chopped celery, chopped capers, sugar, salt, pepper, and then add chopped tomato pulp. Finally swill with wine vinegar and cook under a lid Gas Mark 2 middle shelf until rabbit is delicately tender.

TACCHINO RIPIENO (Milanese Stuffed Turkey)

This appears on diverse feast days. In Italy it is sold prepared at Christmas! We must do it for ourselves.

Ingredients:

1 small 8/9 lb. turkey;

$\frac{1}{4}$ lb. lean veal;

liver of bird;

2 oz. raw ham or gammon;

4 oz. pork sausage meat;

2 small shallots or 1 medium onion;

6 boiled, skinned chestnuts;

4 overnight-soaked prunes (use cold tea to improve flavour);

salt, pepper, nutmeg and 1 oz. grated *Parmesan* cheese;

1 fl. oz. olive oil;

1 large or 2 small eggs.

Method: After prunes have soaked stone them, then place veal and ham (cut into small pieces) in mincer with pepper, shallots, chestnuts, and stoned prunes and mince finely (purists rub this mixture through a fine sieve thereafter). I suggest you merely emulsify with the eggs. Then season with a scant flat teaspoon salt, 1 flat eggspoon pepper, a generous grate of nutmeg and add the grated cheese. If this mixture is rather too thick for your emulsifier or liquidiser add the olive oil too and then, if this makes mixture too flabby, work in a spoonful or two of ground almonds to bring to satisfactory consistency. Fill into bird. Save yourselves hours of messy labour by placing stuffing in a nylon icing bag without any icing pipe affixed and just put narrow filled tip into vent-end and neck end and just squeeze!

For roasting: Rub bird all over with raw, unsalted pork fat which has been previously melted down. Pour 1″ depth of water into baking tin, roast at Gas Mark 4 middle shelf and as soon as breast top has become a light brown, cover this with a piece of aluminium foil for remainder of baking time. Allow 20 minutes for first pound and 15 minutes per pound thereafter.

CARNI

(Meat)

OSSI BUCCHI (Knuckle of Veal)

Ingredients:

3 lb. knuckle of veal cut into 3″ pieces;

seasoned flour;

2 oz. each oil and butter for frying;

3 large carrots diced finely;

1 onion diced finely;

1 small head of celery diced finely;

$\frac{1}{2}$ pint fresh tomato *purée*;

$\frac{1}{4}$ pint *Chianti* or red wine;

1 ladleful stock;

1 leaf of lemon peel;

1 peeled crushed garlic clove;

1 teaspoon chopped fresh basil;

1 teaspoon chopped fresh parsley heads.

Method: Turn meat in seasoned flour. Heat oil and butter together in shallow pan and fry meat briskly. When browned all over, place in casserole. Brown carrots, onion and celery in remaining butter/oil mixture. Tip vegetables into casserole on top of meat and add tomato *purée*, stock and wine. Cover with lid and cook for 1 hour, Gas Mark 4. Then add herbs and lemon peel and cook for further $1\frac{1}{2}$–2 hours. Serve in old-fashioned soup plates.

SALTIMBOCCA (Sauté of Veal, Ham and Sage)

Ingredients:

1 lb. veal, cut by you or the butcher from veal chop (which is the equivalent of beef sirloin) or veal topside (the same as beef topside), and sliced into fairly thick slices;

2 small carrots and 1 medium shallot, or onion, coarsely grated or cut in hair-thin strips *(juliennes)*;

2 fl. oz. oil;

4 oz. butter;

5 fl. oz. dry, white wine;

3 fl. oz. *Marsala;*

7–8 slices Parma or ordinary raw ham;

7–8 large or 14–18 small fresh sage leaves (when possible);

flour;

salt and pepper to season.

Method: Dissolve 2 oz. butter in small pan. Add prepared carrots and onion and fry gently until tender. Bat out veal slices thinly like veal escalopes. Slice into small, neat rectangles. Cut matching slices of chosen ham. Place veal rectangles on working surface. Put 1 or 2 fresh sage leaves on top (when these are unavailable use dried sage and sprinkle lightly over surface). Lay ham rectangles over veal. Secure at centre with ½ a tooth pick or cocktail stick. Sprinkle lightly on both sides with salt and pepper. Turn in flour and dust off surface. Heat oil and 2 oz. butter in large, thick, shallow pan. Lay in prepared veal and ham rectangles, ham side downwards. Step up heat, simmer fiercely for ½ minute. Turn over veal side downwards. Continue simmering for a further 1–1½ minutes, depending upon thickness of veal. Lift portions onto heated dish. Add wine, stock, *Marsala* and fried vegetables. Continue simmering until pan contents thicken to sauce consistency. Remove sticks from *Saltimbocca,* arrange neatly, rub sauce through sieve so that it covers each piece. Arrange a neat oval of plain mashed potatoes at one end and a matching mound of any green vegetable, preferably spinach or green beans, at the other.

Note 1: Remember that veal, like sole, toughens the instant it becomes even slightly over-cooked.

Note 2: If the taste of a touch of lemon juice is acceptable, small ½ slices can be arranged around dish as an edible garnish but this is not classic.

PICCATE DI VITELLO AL MARSALA
(Veal in Marsala)

This, like many of this main course assembly of Italian dishes, is very quickly made and very delightful. We have been driven to buying sides of meat since the terrible rise in prices, and thus can obtain ½ a calf, pig, or lamb, at around 25p per lb. Furthermore we do **not** employ the standard English cuts but have our own, based on the Continental cuts. For example we take $\frac{1}{2}$ head from a calf, then remove the leg and shoulder and cut the belly strip away just short of the rib cage. When this is done we saw through the ribs leaving about 3″ only attached to the length of loin. These are gorgeous when treated in any of the ways for pork spare ribs. We then chine our loin pieces, which enables us to cut leaf-thin, smallish slices from the chop/cutlet flesh. If these are then batted out with a meat batter (or old, cleaned, flat iron), dipped into cold water, they are far the easiest way of obtaining the kind of meat used for *Piccate, Saltimbocca* and suchlike. Turning this explanation round to suit a piece of loin of pork bought from the butcher, whom you can ask to chine it for you if you wish; you can do the same either at the current high prices, or do the whole job yourself at much reduced prices if you can share/buy a whole side. So if you wish, you can by-pass our ingredient instructions for divided veal escalopes, cut slivers from the narrow end of a loin, and bat them out, using the rest for a roast.

Ingredients:

16 very very thin $2\frac{1}{2}$″ to 3″ trimmed squares of tender veal *(escalope?)*;

salt, pepper;

flour;

lemon juice;

$1\frac{1}{2}$ oz. each of butter and olive oil;

$2\frac{1}{2}$ fl. oz. *Marsala*;

$2\frac{1}{2}$ fl. oz. white meat or chicken stock (well reduced to give full flavour).

Method: Dissolve butter with oil and raise until it sizzles over a moderate heat. Season each piece of veal with a pinch of salt and pepper, give a squeeze of lemon juice and then turn in sifted flour. Dust off the surplus and slide into the hot pan mixture. Brown quickly on each side, add the *Marsala,* allow this to come to a bubble and then add the stock. Bubble up once more, cover with a lid and allow to simmer gently for an absolute maximum of 2 minutes. Lift out the veal and arrange on a heated dish. Stir pan liquor/residue, re-bubble until syrupy, strain over veal and serve with additional lemon segments if desired.

BOCCONCINI (Veal and Ham Rolls)

Ingredients:

3 veal *escalopes*;

3 thin slices cooked ham;

six $\frac{1}{2}$″ thick fingers of *Gruyère* or *Emmenthal* cheese;

fresh sage leaves (optional);

$1\frac{1}{2}$ fl. oz. oil;

1 oz. butter;

2 fl. oz. dry white wine;

4 fl. oz. veal or pork stock;

1 flat tablespoon concentrated tomato *purée*;

salt and pepper to season.

Method: Bat out *escalopes* very thinly indeed, then halve them centrally, making 6, and halve the ham slices. Lay ham on veal, covering each piece with a small sage leaf; lay a finger of cheese down each centrally. Roll up and secure with a wooden (never plastic!) cocktail stick. Melt butter and heat with oil in a shallow, thick pan; place little rolls in pan over moderate heat and brown all over. Add remaining ingredients. Reduce heat and simmer until veal is tender, turning occasionally. Lift out, arrange in heated container. Simmer sauce in pan until thick and creamy; taste; season with salt and pepper and pour same overall.

VITELLO ALLA SARDA
(Veal with Garlic, Anchovies etc.)

Ingredients:

4 anchovy fillets from oil not brine!;

1 crushed garlic clove;

3 lb. bone-less loin of veal;

2 fl. oz. olive oil;

8 small black olives, peeled and cut into small slivers;

given quantity *Salsa di Pomodoro* (p. 82);

salt and pepper to season;

1 teaspoon strained lemon juice;

2 heaped tablespoons fresh, milled parsley;

4 oz. peeled, finely chopped onions;

3 oz. finely chopped celery heart;

4 oz. finely chopped carrots;

8 fl. oz. veal or chicken stock;

4 fl. oz. inexpensive, dry, white Italian wine.

Method: Chop anchovy fillets, work garlic with 1 rounded tablespoon parsley, turn anchovy pieces in this well blended mixture. Then drive $\frac{1}{2}''$ incisions into the veal joint and insert the prepared anchovy pieces. Heat oil in a large, shallow pan and brown meat over a brisk heat turning as you work. Lift out joint and set aside. Add to pan residue, the onion, carrot, and celery, stir and cook until lightly browned being careful to stir. After 7 minutes maximum add wine, raise heat to high and stir/cook for 3/4 minutes. Turn into a casserole. Lay veal on this vegetable bed. Add stock, cover with a lid and cook slowly 1 shelf below centre at Gas Mark 3/4 until meat is tender. Then remove meat, add *Salsa di Pomodoro,* and prepared olives, stir well. Taste and correct seasoning with salt, pepper and lemon juice. Re-cover and return to oven, Gas Mark 6, 1 shelf above centre, for 7 minutes. Then slice meat and either serve from the pot, or arrange slices on a heated dish, pour sauce/vegetable mixture overall and sprinkle remaining parsley on top.

VITELLO TONNATO (Veal with Tuna)

Ingredients:

2 lb. boned leg or fillet of veal;

8 fl. oz. water;

2 separated egg yolks;

salt and pepper to season;

4 fl. oz. olive oil;

the strained juice from ¼ of a lemon;

2 oz. pounded-to-paste tuna fish.

Method: Brush the chosen veal with a little extra olive oil, place in a meat baking tin with a very light covering of kitchen foil. Roast at Gas Mark 6 until veal is just tender. Remove meat, leave to cool and pour any surplus fat from pan. Place pan over low flame, add water and stir quickly until mixture bubbles, pour into small container and leave until cold. Whip egg yolks with fish until they form a thick paste, add a pinch of salt, a pinch of pepper and the olive oil very gradually, whipping all the time. When mixture is really stiff, add lemon juice, whip again and finally, whip in the cold pan liquor. Slice up the cold veal, arrange on a flat dish, cover with the tuna fish mayonnaise and serve with a green salad.

SPEZZATINO DI VITELLO (Veal Casserole)

Ingredients:

1¼ lb. lean pie veal;

6 oz. onions;

2 oz. raw, unsalted pork fat;

a little seasoned flour;

1 large pimento;

4 oz. skinned, cored, de-seeded, tomato flesh;

4 fl. oz. inexpensive, dry, white Italian wine;

salt and pepper to season;

8 fl. oz. well-reduced pork bone stock;

8 oz. shelled, fresh peas (optional).

Method: Cut the meat into neat, small-ish pieces, turn these in flour, dust off surplus. Melt the pork fat in a thick, shallow pan over a low heat. Increase heat to medium strength and fry veal pieces briskly until browned all over. Lift out and lay in a small casserole. In pan residue fry thinly sliced onions, after 5 minutes add de-seeded strips of pimento, from which every scrap of inner white pith has been removed. After a further 2 minutes, add tomato flesh, fry for a further minute, swill with the wine, stir well. Dilute with ½ the given stock, allow mixture to bubble up then turn over meat in casserole. Sprinkle very lightly with pepper, fairly liberally with salt, cover and cook, 1 shelf below centre, at Gas Mark 3 for 1¾ hours.

If the time of year permits you to use fresh peas, add these and stir them in, with as much of the stock as you find necessary, 30 minutes before the end of your cooking time.

SFORMATO DI VITELLO O MAIALE E ZUCCHINI (Veal or Pork with Baby Marrows)

Note: In the interests of economy we are giving the recipe for pork. In fact, veal or lamb may be used instead.

Ingredients:

1 lb. lean pork cut into small, thin slices;

1 lb. baby marrows (ideally *Zucchini*);

one 4″ piece un-skinned cucumber;

salt;

pepper;

$3\frac{1}{2}$ oz. coarsely grated *Parmesan* cheese;

nutmeg;

a little butter.

Method: Slice the unskinned chosen marrow and cucumber into $\frac{1}{4}″$ rounds, spread out in a shallow dish. Sprinkle with salt and leave for about 50 minutes. Then rub a deep-ish medium pie dish with butter, put in $\frac{1}{2}$ the marrow slices and season with pepper and finely grated nutmeg sprinkled very lightly. Cover with $\frac{1}{4}$ of the pork, 1 or 2 tiny flakes of butter, and $\frac{1}{4}$ of the cheese. Then add $\frac{1}{2}$ the cucumber, season with nutmeg and pepper as explained, then the second $\frac{1}{4}$ of meat, then second $\frac{1}{4}$ of cheese, then repeat, alternating remaining marrow, meat, cheese, cucumber, meat, cheese, ending with cheese. Top this with generous flakes of butter well-distributed over top surface. Place in oven, 1 shelf below centre, at Gas Mark 4 and cook without any covering for 40/45 minutes. Serve piping hot.

COSTE DI MAIALE (Pork Spare Ribs)

Ingredients:

Required number of pork spare ribs;

olive oil.
Salsa Pizzaiola (p. 85).

Method: We prefer our pork spare ribs crisp and browned, so we just brush them very lightly with olive oil, place them in an ordinary meat baking tin and bake at Gas Mark 5/6 for 35/45 minutes. Allow less time if spare ribs are meanly covered with meat. Alternatively, you can brush them with olive oil and lay them on a grill rack. Place rack at low position and turn when cooked on upper side. Eat with your fingers, dunking spare ribs into sauce and please do not forget finger bowls!

COSTOLETTE DI MAIALE ALLA
MODENESE (Pork Cutlets with Wine and Herbs)

Although this, in its correct Italian form, is a recipe for Pork Cutlets we have also used it with pork ribs and it made a highly successful more economical dish!

Ingredients:

1 rounded teaspoon each of fresh finely milled or chopped sage and of fresh parsley heads and pounded rosemary spikes;

1 flat teaspoon salt;

1 medium to small garlic clove peeled and crushed;

1 flat eggspoon pepper;

1 oz. butter;

1 fl. oz. olive oil;

6 fl. oz. dry-ish Italian white wine;

8 small, trimmed pork cutlets.

Method: Mix the garlic, rosemary and sage with the pepper. Spread over the raw cutlets. Melt butter and heat oil in a shallow pan and when thoroughly hot slip in the cutlets and brown briskly on both sides. Reduce heat to low. Pour all but a surface coating of butter/oil off the pan (and use again), and do this through a strainer so as to return to the pan any little 'driftwood' of herbs and garlic. Add the wine, cover with a lid or with aluminium foil and simmer gently until cutlets are tender (approximately 25/30 minutes). Remove cutlets onto heated serving dish and keep warm. Raise heat once more to brisk and allow mixture to bubble and reduce while working down pan particles with the back of a wooden spoon, until fluid has become syrupy. Taste, correct seasoning, stir in prepared parsley, pour carefully over cutlets and serve at once.

COSTOLETTE DI MAIALE ALLA
PIZZAIOLA (Pork Cutlets with Garlic and Tomatoes)

This has been, in our experience, one of the most outstandingly successful dishes made with pork cutlets.

Ingredients:

6 pork cutlets;

double the quantity of *Salsa Pizzaiolo* (p. 85);

6 fl. oz. inexpensive, red Italian wine;

2 fl. oz. olive oil;

salt and pepper to season.

Method: Heat the oil in a thick, shallow pan and trim the cutlets neatly. When the oil is hot, brown the cutlets on both sides over a fairly brisk heat, lift them out. Pour the wine into the pan residue, step up the heat and reduce, by allowing mixture to bubble while stirring, to $\frac{1}{2}$ its original quantity. Add the *Salsa Pizzaiola,* stir again, when this bubbles sink in the browned cutlets, cover and cook over a low heat, basting occasionally, for 40 minutes. Remember this last cooking stage **must** be done very gently. Season to taste with salt and pepper.

ARISTA FIORENTINA (Florentine Roast Pork)

Note: For this it is essential to use loin of pork!

Ingredients:

one 3 to 4 lb. piece of loin of pork;

2 garlic cloves;

one 2″ long stem of fresh rosemary;

1 flat teaspoon salt;

1 flat eggspoon black pepper;

water.

Method: Unlike the English, the Italians always remove the rind from pork to be cooked in this manner. Then, should the upper part under the skin have an excessive amount of fat, remove sufficient fat with a very sharp knife to leave a maximum $\frac{1}{4}″$ thickness of top-fat. Refrigerate the rest for using as required. It will refrigerate for 1 week or freeze indefinitely if left on the rind, rolled up and slipped into a polythene bag before freezing. Peel the garlic cloves, cut into slivers and drive at intervals into the fatty top down its length using the tip of a very small, pointed kitchen knife. Strip the rosemary stem of its spikes, pound down to a paste with the salt and pepper. Spread/press the resultant paste over the garlic-studded top. Place in a meat baking tin. Pour boiling water around the sides to a depth of 1″. Place in the oven at Gas Mark 4, middle shelf, and at this slow-roasting time allow 3 hours for a 4 lb. piece of pork or 2 hours for a 3 lb. piece. Remove pan from oven and allow to become cold in remaining liquor. A fatty crust will form on top. Trim this away round the joint and serve cold. Strain off the liquor, reserving the fat for future use. Place liquor in a pan, reduce by simmering to 2 fl. oz. Then chill and, when cold, beat into $\frac{1}{4}$ pint classic mayonnaise. Hand this separately with chosen salads (p. 89).

BISTECCA ALLA FIORENTINA

(T. Bone Steak cooked in the manner of Florence)

This is more of an explanation than a recipe, for few of us can raise either a charcoal fire or large T bone steaks these days. Moreover, if you wish to be purists about this famous dish, the steaks must be taken from young beef, ideally of about 2 years old! Then when the grid over the glowing bed of charcoal is really hot you lay on the steaks, which should make a rude swearing sound on impact – and grill on both sides to rare (red inside), medium (pink inside) or well-done (a synonym for ruined!). Whenever we have eaten them in Florence they have been served with a dish of white beans on the side, soaked, cooked in stock and dressed with oil and vinegar.

STUFATO DI MANZO (Stewing Steak)

Ingredients:

2 lb. uncut lean stewing steak;

2 lb. peeled-weight sliced and then diced onions;

8 oz. firm, skinned tomatoes;

6 oz. carrot (without cores);

2 stems of white celery;

2 oz. butter;

2 fl. oz. olive oil;

6 fl. oz. dry, white wine;

6 fl. oz. strongly reduced beef bone stock;

salt and pepper to season;

3 basil leaves, chopped finely.

Method: Scrape carrots and halve lengthwise and unless they are very young ones, cut out the yellow central core, then slice to achieve given weight. Chop celery finely too. Heat oil with butter and when 'singing' slide in the onions and cook over a very low heat until tender, but not brown. Strain soft onions, allowing fat to fall back into pan. Set onions in base of medium sized casserole, just sufficiently large to accommodate piece of meat. Fry the whole piece of beef over a brisk heat for 1 minute on each side to seal. Place in casserole on top of onion bed. Slice the tomatoes and strew over top, add carrot, celery, a generous seasoning of salt and pepper and then the basil. Pour wine and stock over meat. Cover and cook, 1 shelf below centre, Gas Mark 2, for 2–3 hours or until everything is tender. Then either serve from the pot or slice into convenient pieces. Set on a heated plate for a moment. Arrange liquor and vegetables on a dish, place the meat on top and send to table.

BISTECCA ALLA PIZZAIOLA (Rump Steak)

This is a Neapolitan dish cooked with tomato and garlic.

Ingredients for 4:

Four 6/8 oz. rump steaks;

1 lb. 6 oz. (peeled weight) ripe tomatoes;

2 small sprigs oregano or 4 large, very finely chopped fresh basil

leaves;

3 fl. oz. olive oil;

4 small, peeled, crushed, garlic cloves.

Method: Think of someone you do not really like but are too nicely brought up to tell them what you think of them and take it out on the 4 steaks with a rolling pin protected by a clean teacloth. 'Sock' them, then season lightly on both sides with salt and pepper. Place 2 fl. oz. of given oil in a small pan and heat. Add the rough chopped tomatoes, generous seasoning of salt and pepper and the garlic pulp. Stir over a moderate heat for just long enough to achieve a blending; but not of a totally pulped sauce consistency. Add oregano or basil. Place remaining 1 oz. oil in a roomy frying pan. Heat until it begins to sing, slide in the steaks, turn up the heat and seal them briskly on both sides. Spread the sauce evenly over the 4 upper surfaces after so doing, allowing some of it to fall into the base of the pan. Cover with a lid or double fold of heavy-duty freezer aluminium foil. Reduce the heat to fairly low. Cook for another 5 minutes and serve.

COSTOLETTE D'AGNELLO

(Best End Neck of Lamb)

These, which are perfectly delicious, were new to us until we started our recent Italian cookery research and are immensely popular with all our brood.

Ingredients:

1 best end neck of lamb, chined and divided into single cutlets;

three 2″ sprigs fresh rosemary;

5 fl. oz. dry, white cooking wine or 2½ fl. oz. each of wine and lamb bone stock;

the strained juice of ½ a large lemon;

salt and pepper to season;

1 oz. butter;

1 fl. oz. olive oil;

1 large peeled, crushed garlic clove.

Method: Dissolve butter and heat with oil in a frying pan. Fry cutlets briskly on both sides for about 1 minute per side, remove and reduce heat under pan to very low indeed. Strip the 'spikes' from the rosemary and either chop very finely or pound in a mortar with a pestle, then work into pan juices with the back of a wooden spoon together with the prepared garlic and a seasoning of both salt and pepper. Next, work in the lemon juice then the wine or wine and stock, return cutlets to this well-blended mixture, cover lightly with kitchen foil and simmer with extreme gentleness for 15 minutes. Turn cutlets, simmer for a further 15 minutes. Arrange cutlets on a heated dish, with or without benefit of cutlet frills, pour pan liquor overall and serve.

ABBACCHIO BRODETTATTO

(Shoulder of Lamb)

This is an excellent Italian casserole which we often use for family meals.

Ingredients:

one 3½ lb. lean-as-possible shoulder of lamb;

2 oz. raw, diced, unsalted pork fat;

salt and pepper to season;

4 fl. oz. dry, white wine (or substitute this extra quantity of well-reduced bone stock);

1 large, peeled, crushed garlic clove;

1½ pints well-reduced bone stock;

1 torn bay leaf;

2 separated egg yolks;

1 tablespoon strained lemon juice;

2 rounded tablespoons fresh, milled or finely chopped, parsley heads;

seasoned flour.

Method: Heat a thick (ideally iron) frying pan over a moderate heat, toss in the pork fat dice and shake/stir briskly until the fat runs and the dice become shrivelled and brown. Remove these leaving only the fat in the pan. Trim off surplus fat as desired from lamb and then cut the rest away from the bone. Cut this meat into 1¼"–1½" chunks, turn in seasoned flour, dust off surplus and fry briskly until browned all over in the pan fat. Remove to a casserole. Stir garlic into remaining pan residue, pour in the 4 fl. oz. wine or extra stock, bubble up strongly and reduce to a mere pan-coating, working the while with the back of a wooden spoon to incorporate all the flavoursome scraps clinging to the pan's base and sides. Then work in remaining stock and torn bayleaf, allow to heat through and then pour over meat pieces in casserole. Cover with a lid and cook in the oven for 1½ hours at Gas Mark 4. Remove meat and keep warm. Strain liquor into the top of a double saucepan over hot water. Run a piece or two of tissue paper over top surface to remove any surplus fat – such an easy way which can also be done with absorbent kitchen paper! Beat egg yolks and lemon juice together and work in 2 tablespoons of hot stock, pour mixture into pan with remaining stock, and stir until sauce thickens. By doing this in a double or porage saucepan there is no possible risk of the egg yolks curdling. Taste, correct seasoning if desired with salt and pepper and pour sauce over lamb in chosen dish. Sprinkle parsley overall and serve.

FEGATO ALLA VENEZIANA

(Calves Liver with Onions)

There is a rather naughty but money-saving trick for substituting ox liver. Slice this, slide into a small bowl of milk, using just enough to cover. Leave overnight. Drain milk away which will now look and taste disgusting and liver will be found to have thus been lightened in colour and tenderised.

Ingredients:

1 lb. liver cut into $\frac{1}{4}''$ strips;

4 tablespoons olive oil;

4 oz. very thinly sliced onions;

2 crumbled (medium) dried sage leaves;

salt and pepper;

1 tablespoon white wine vinegar;

2 tablespoons finely chopped or milled fresh parsley heads.

Method: Heat 2 tablespoons of given oil in a thick, shallow pan. Add onions and cook over medium heat, turning and shaking occasionally as you do so for a maximum 8 minutes. Stir in sage and cook for 4 minutes more, then set aside. Dry liver strips, spread onto working surface, sprinkle lightly with both salt and pepper. Heat remaining oil in same pan and then add liver strips over fairly brisk heat. Turn and stir until lightly browned all over. Stir in onion mixture and continue cooking for 3 minutes. Transfer pan contents to heated dish and keep warm. Put vinegar into pan and stir to collect residue juices and blend them in. Simmer gently for 1 minute, stir in parsley and pour over liver and onions. Serve immediately.

FRITTO MISTO

(Tiny pieces of Meat, Offal and Vegetables fried in Batter)

Fritto Misto is almost a generic in Italy. It can, and should be a delight, but in many restaurants and some homes it becomes a sad, soggy mess. This can only happen if each little item is dipped and fried well in advance of service and kept warm until each becomes flabby, or if the wrong batter is used.

Ingredients:

Proper fritter batter;*

hot oil for deep-frying;

cut lemons;

tiny pieces of – veal *escalope,* chickens' breasts, blanched sweetbreads;** *Mozzarella* cheese; plus 3 or many more of the following items:—

blanched lambs' brains, plus 2 or 3 vegetable items such as slices of unskinned aubergine (egg plant;*** de-stalked mushrooms, tiny Italian artichoke hearts, little flowerets cut from the white of cauliflower and steamed until cooked but still firm, marrow, courgette or zucchini flowers.

Method: Dip each prepared item into fritter batter. Deep fry until puffy and pale golden brown at 375°F so as to allow time for cooking right through without the batter becoming dark brown. Pile on a napkin-covered dish and optionally sprinkle lightly with paprika powder. Border with pieces of cut lemon and serve immediately.

Note: With all items pre-prepared and everything set to hand, this does not involve the cook in anything more than very brief last minute cookery.

*Fritter Batter

Ingredients:

4 heaped tablespoons flour;
2 tablespoons olive oil;
1 separated egg white;

1 generous pinch of salt;
7 fl. oz. cold water.

Method: Place flour and salt in a roomy bowl, make a well in the centre, put in the oil, add about ⅓ of the given water and beat until absolutely smooth. Beat in the remaining water, cover and leave for 2 hours before dipping and frying. Then at the last moment, when oil is hot and all ingredients are assembled, beat in the stiffly whipped egg white. Turn each item in the batter, allow surplus to drip off and slide into the hot oil to fry.

**How to Blanch Sweetbreads or Brains

Put 2 rounded tablespoons of flour into a small bowl, stir to a smooth paste with gradual additions of cold water. Pour on boiling water, slowly stirring all the while until the mixture clears – just like making starch! Immerse the chosen items, after washing and, in the case of brains, removing the red veins. Bring *blanc,* as it is called by professionals, back to boiling point. Simmer for 1 minute and leave sweetbreads or brains in until mixture has become completely cold. Drain, wipe and use.

***Preparation of Aubergines

Cut away stem from each egg plant, cut into rounds a generous ⅛″ in thickness and arrange them over a wooden board. Sprinkle liberally with salt and leave until the salt has become an unattractive brown fluid. Wipe each slice, dip in batter and fry.

VERDURE

(Vegetables)

CAROTE AL MARSALA (Carrots)

Ingredients:

2 lb. prepared-weight carrots;

1 oz. butter;

salt and black pepper to season;

1 rounded teaspoon castor sugar;

4 fl. oz. *Marsala*;

½ pint ordinary stock;

1 flat dessertspoon milled fresh parsley heads.

Method: Scrape carrots and halve lengthwise. Cut out the pale hard cores or centres then slice and weigh to achieve given quantity. Dissolve butter in a thick saucepan or sauté pan. Add prepared carrots. Turn them well so that they become thoroughly impregnated with butter, then season with salt, black pepper and sugar and turn again over a moderate heat for 2 minutes. Swill with *Marsala,* simmer on for a further 4 minutes. Swill with given stock. Cover and simmer very gently until tender. Then turn up the heat, remove the lid and stir/turn with a wooden spoon while the pan liquor reduces to a mere coating of dark syrup. Turn into a serving dish, sprinkle with given parsley and serve.

SPINACH PUREE (how to make)

Place 1 lb. well picked and stalked, washed spinach leaves in an absolutely dry pan. Stir occasionally over an extremely moderate heat until spinach has vastly collapsed and juices run freely. Then cook on, limiting overall cooking time to 7 minutes. Rub through a sieve with own juices and use.

FINOCCHI DI FIRENZE (Florentine Fennel)

This comes from the 3-in-1 plant which yields such long and feathery fronds to use in flower arrangements. It is the special herb for fish cookery and grows from a corm (a fat root of ridged, layered petals which pack closely one over the other). This is the part you cook and serve as a vegetable.

Ingredients:

2 large or 4 small bulbous bases of Florentine fennel;

water to cover;

2 large lemons;

melted butter;

grated *Parmesan* cheese;

1 rounded teaspoon salt.

Method: Detach the stained hard outer leaves which are slightly greenish, then detach the white ones and cut the layer ones into strips. Either scrape or peel all these – whichever you find easiest – and as you do each one rub it all over with cut lemon and toss into cold water to cover which has been mixed with the strained juice of the second lemon and salt. Steep in this mixture for 15 minutes, wipe and slip into a fluid composed of flour and water. Stir 1 heaped tablespoon flour to a paste with cold water. Pour on boiling water and stir until smooth and slightly thick. Use 2 pints of boiling water altogether. Cover with a lid and cook with extreme gentleness until tender, i.e. a minimum 1 hour. Then drain and pile up into chosen serving dish. As you build up sprinkle each layer with melted butter and grated *Parmesan* cheese and when all are so treated sprinkle more grated cheese liberally over the top, add a few flakes of additional butter and brown fast under a brisk grill.

GNOCCHI DI PATATE (Potato Cakes)

Ingredients:

2½ lb. peeled potatoes;

1½ oz. butter;

2 separated egg yolks;

5 oz. sifted flour;

salt, pepper and grated nutmeg to season;

4 oz. *Emmenthal* or *Gruyère* cheese;

a little extra grated cheese;

butter.

Method: Steam the potatoes, drain thoroughly and sieve. Work in the butter and egg yolks, then flour, and correct seasoning with salt and pepper. Weigh off into ½ oz. pieces, roll these into little balls and then flatten them a little with the back of a fork. Two-thirds fill a roomy pan with slightly salted water and raise to simmering point. Drop in *Gnocchi* and remove **as each one rises** to the surface. Butter a shallow, heat-resistant dish and arrange the *Gnocchi* in layers with generous sprinklings of cheese and butter between each layer. Brush top surface with melted butter and cheese. When required (they can wait overnight in refrigeration), bake at Gas Mark 4, 1 shelf above centre for 30 minutes.

CROCCHETTE DI SPINACI (Spinach Croquettes)

This recipe makes 9 croquettes.

Ingredients:

¾ lb. picked weight, well washed spinach;

2 oz. *Parmesan* cheese;

1 egg;

2 oz. soft, fine, brown or white breadcrumbs;

salt, black pepper and nutmeg to season;

a shallow container of sifted flour;

another containing 1 raw, beaten, strained egg;

and a third of fine, soft, brown or white breadcrumbs.

Method: Place the prepared spinach, without any water, in a roomy pan and allow to collapse over medium heat, stirring if leaves tend to adhere at the beginning to sides of pan. Cook for a maximum 7 minutes, press through an ordinary sieve to expel surplus juices, then chop spinach fairly finely. Scrape into a bowl, work in cheese, well-beaten egg, salt, pepper and nutmeg to taste and finally the breadcrumbs. Shape into little rissoles. Turn in container of flour and dust off surplus, pass through raw, beaten egg and drain off surplus. Bury in breadcrumbs and pat in very thoroughly. At this stage re-shape if necessary. Set all in the frying basket of your deep fryer containing hot oil. Heat oil to 385°F, level bottom heat at medium, plunge in basket of croquettes and shake handle of fryer basket to maintain seethe and keep croquettes browning evenly all over. When nicely brown, turn on to absorbent kitchen paper for a moment to drain and they are ready for service.

FUNGHI O PEPERONE RIPIENI
(Stuffed Mushrooms)

Ingredients:

6 large mushroom flats, or 2 hollowed out pimentoes, approx. diameter 4″, and their stalks;

2 oz. cooked, diced, lean ham or bacon scraps;

2 oz. coarsely grated *Parmesan* or hard Cheddar cheese;

1 rounded teaspoon fresh, milled parsley heads;

1 peeled, crushed garlic clove;

2 tablespoons thick, plain, unseasoned, basic white sauce;

a little oil;

a pinch of nutmeg;

salt and pepper.

Method: Mix chopped mushroom stalks, diced ham and grated cheese with parsley and salt and pepper. Fold crushed garlic and pinch of nutmeg into white sauce, taste, correct seasoning with salt and pepper. Bind dry mixture with sauce. When thoroughly blended dome over unskinned, just scalded, mushrooms, which have been placed on a heat-resistant platter, flick drips of olive oil over the tops. Bake under a light tenting of oiled kitchen foil in the oven at Gas Mark 4, middle shelf, for 25/30 minutes. Serve piping hot.

Note: The reference to 'flats' may confuse young, inexperienced cooks. These are 3 standard categories of English mushrooms, which are what we must use unless we are experienced in identifying the wild funghi which are poisonous from the ones which are NOT! These categories are – Button, Cup and Flat. The first are the small, tight ones where the rim of the mushroom meets the central stalk. The second are the ½-opened cup-like ones and the third are the wide-open, black undersided, biggest of all, ones.

TORTA DI PATATE (Potato Pie)

Ingredients:

1 lb. peeled-weight steamed, sieved, old potatoes;

2 oz. *Gruyère, Emmenthal* or *Bel Paese* cheese;

1 oz. cooked, lean ham;

2 hard boiled eggs;

2 heaped tablespoons fine, soft, white or brown breadcrumbs (the latter are not current usage in Italy remember!);

nutmeg;

salt and pepper;

a little butter.

Method: Rub the interior base and sides of a 6–6½″ diameter soufflé mould with butter. Sprinkle buttery surface with 1 tablespoon of given breadcrumbs. Add a walnut of butter, a generous pinch of nutmeg, and salt and pepper to taste, to the hot, sieved potatoes. Spread $\frac{1}{2}$ this mixture into the mould. Level off the top. Cover with the shelled and coarsely chopped, hard-boiled eggs. Season again with salt and pepper, cover with chosen cheese sliced extremely thinly. Cover with the diced ham. Pack in remaining potatoes, season once more with salt and pepper, spread remaining breadcrumbs on top, moisten liberally with melted butter and bake in the oven at Gas Mark 6, 1 shelf above centre, for 20/25 minutes until nicely browned on top and piping hot inside. Serve immediately.

ZUCCHINI IN AGRODOLCE

(*Zucchini* or Baby Marrows)

These are really delectable.

Ingredients:

1 lb. *Zucchini*;	black pepper, powdered cinnamon;
salt;	1 oz. wine vinegar;
1 fl. oz. olive oil;	1 rounded tablespoon soft brown (pieces) sugar.

Method: Chop off stem and tiny flower end tips from all *zucchini* then slice into $\frac{1}{8}''$ rounds. Heat oil, slide in sliced *zucchini*, cover pan and give a vigorous shake from time to time until they reach the almost tender stage. Remove lid, season to taste with salt, pepper and cinnamon. Turn well, add vinegar and sugar and keep turning until you achieve a smooth coating of the fluid content.

PARMIGIANA (Egg Plant or Aubergine)

Ingredients:

1 fat, firm shiny 9 oz. egg plant or aubergine;	2 fl. oz. *Salsa Pizzaiola* (p. 85);
2 oz. *Mozzarella* cheese;	3 fl. oz. olive oil;
$\frac{1}{4}$ oz. finely grated *Parmesan* cheese;	salt and black pepper and a very little flour.

Method: Peel aubergine very finely and cut into 'twiggy' strips. Sprinkle all over with salt on a wooden surface (chopping board) and cover with clean cloth; leave for 1 hour. Wipe well; sprinkle lightly with flour and turn until thinly coated, adding more flour if necessary. Heat oil in frying pan until it 'sings', slide in prepared 'twigs', fry over moderate heat for 3–4 minutes maximum. Drain on absorbent kitchen paper. Oil a very small soufflé mould or similar item, cover base meanly with 'twigs', cover with $\frac{1}{3}$ of paper-thinly sliced *Mozzarella* (substitute *Bel Paese*). Moisten with $\frac{1}{3}$ sauce, repeat twice more; scatter *Parmesan* on top; moisten with teaspoon or 2 of residue oil from frying pan. Bake Gas No. 4 middle shelf for 30 minutes.

CAPONATA (Egg Plant or Aubergine)

Ingredients:

18 oz. fat, hard, shiny egg plant;

1 flattish dessertspoon pressed capers;

1½ oz. peeled, small green olives;

1 small tight head celery chopped finely;

2 anchovy fillets wiped and chopped finely;

2 small shallots or 1 small/medium onion thinly sliced;

¾ oz. castor or soft brown (pieces) sugar;

1 generous tablespoon concentrated tomato *purée* diluted with 2 fl. oz. ordinary bone stock;

3 fl. oz. real wine vinegar;

salt and black pepper;

1 rounded dessertspoon milled fresh parsley heads;

oil in deep fryer;

1 small 7 oz. tuna fish in oil.

Method: Peel egg plants extremely finely, cut into fat cubes, set on chopping board, sprinkle liberally with coarse salt *(Gros sel* or Rock), cover with cloth, leave 1 hour then wipe thoroughly. Toss into oil heated to 380°F (15°F below smoking), cook through, lift out, drain on absorbent kitchen paper. Steal a couple of tablespoons hot oil from fryer and fry onions in this in shallow pan until tender but not brown. Add chosen sugar and tomato *purée* mixed with stock. Simmer fast for about 2½ minutes, add vinegar and simmer on for 4 minutes. Correct seasoning to taste with salt and pepper and stir in parsley, capers, celery, anchovies, olives and the now cooled egg plant. Arrange on a dish in a mound. Flake tuna fish in its own oil, use as a surrounding border and serve either as an accompanying vegetable to cold meat or as part of an hors d'oeuvre assembly.

FRITTO MISTO DI VERDURE

(Mixed Vegetables in Batter)

Ingredients:

1 small egg plant;

two 3½"–4" *Zucchini*;

8 vegetable marrow flowers;

fritter batter (p. 67);

Mozzarella or *Bel Paese* cheese.

Method: Try to choose a fat rather round egg plant. Cut from top to bottom in ¼" thick slices. Sprinkle all over with salt on a wooden chopping board and cover with clean cloth. Leave for 1 hour then wipe well. Do the same with the unpeeled *zucchini*. Remove pistils and all stems from marrow flowers. Just before serving, slide each prepared item through the fritter batter, slide into deep fryer of hot oil 380°F over moderate heat. Drain on absorbent kitchen paper then optionally scatter with a few finely chopped basil leaves mixed with a little extra grated *Parmesan* cheese or powdered paprika. Serve fast.

ASPARAGI ALLA FIORENTINA
(Asparagus in Florentine manner)

Ingredients:

1 lb. trimmed, scraped, cooked asparagus;

3 oz. butter;

salt;

milled black pepper;

1 oz. grated *Parmesan* cheese;

4 eggs.

Method: Drain cooked asparagus very thoroughly. Melt given butter in large shallow pan. When this sizzles slide in asparagus and turn carefully over a brisk heat until well impregnated. Drain again, set on a warmed dish in 4 equal portions. Set heat under pan at low. Break eggs into remaining butter in pan and cook gently until set, spooning butter over yolks to give a fine white film. Lift out and set over 4 bunches asparagus. Season lightly with salt, fairly strongly with black pepper, sprinkle with cheese and serve immediately.

PISELLI AL PROSCIUTTO (Peas with Ham)

Ingredients:

1 lb. shelled young peas;

1 oz. melted, strained, raw, unsalted pork fat;

3 tablespoons very well reduced white bone or chicken stock;

3 oz. raw, thinly-sliced Italian ham *(prosciutto)*;

black pepper to season.

Method: Tip peas into a casserole. Pour on the melted fat and the stock. Cut ham into matchsticks. Stir in, season with pepper, cover with lid and cook very gently, Gas Mark 3 middle shelf until peas are tender. Serve from casserole in own liquor which is delicious!

FAGIOLI ASSOLUTI (Kidney Beans)

Ingredients:

½ lb. dried beans;

water;

2 fl. oz. olive oil;

1 crushed garlic clove;

1 rounded tablespoon fresh,
  milled parsley heads;

2 fat parsley stalks;

1 sprig marjoram;

2 pinches of cayenne pepper;

a further generous pinch white
  pepper;

salt.

Method: Soak beans overnight in cold water. Drain, place in pan with cold water to cover fairly generously, parsley and marjoram stalks, first stripped of their leaves. Add a rounded teaspoon of salt and simmer until tender, then drain thoroughly. Heat oil in shallow pan until it 'sings'. Slide in beans, garlic, parsley, milled marjoram leaves and both peppers. Turn over moderate heat until well-impregnated.

UOVA E FORMAGGI

(Eggs and Cheese)

MOZZARELLA IN CARROZZA

(Italian version of French *Croque M'sieu*)

Mozzarella can be replaced by *Bel Paese* if desired.

Ingredients:

Desired quantity of crustless bread, each piece to measure $3'' \times 2'' \times \frac{1}{8}''$ in thickness;

thin matching sized strips of *Mozzarella** cheese or substitute;

1 or more eggs;

deep fryer of hot oil;

a little butter.

Method: Butter bread fingers in pairs. Make into sandwiches with chosen cheese in between. Whip egg or eggs. Pass 'sandwiches' through and leave to soak until well impregnated but not collapsed! Drain, slide into smoking hot oil and fry briskly until richly golden brown all over thus giving cheese time to melt and become gooey and delicious. Optionally garnish a pile with fried sprigs of well washed, dried parsley heads. These need only seconds in the hot oil to become crisp and highly edible!

*Mozzarella is obtainable from Parmigiani, 43 Frith Street, Soho, London. Tel. 01-437 4728.

TORTA DI BLEIA (Cold Egg and Veal Cake)

This is a most unusual dish, very useful for serving with salads or indeed at any cold buffet. *Bleia* – a distant relation of spinach – is generally unobtainable in Britain which is highly regrettable as it comprises 2 vegetables in 1. The leaves are used as spinach and the long fat white stems which are generally treated like celeriac or cardoon.

Ingredients:

6 eggs;	1 oz. butter;
3 oz. grated *Parmesan* cheese;	4 oz. minced, lean veal;
1 teacupful sieved dry, cooked, spinach rough-chopped;	salt and pepper to season.

Method: Butter a straight-sided earthenware casserole very generously. Whip up eggs, add cheese, spinach and veal. Beat up fairly evenly with a fork, season with salt and pepper. Pour into prepared container, cover with foil and lid, and cook at Gas Mark 2 until set (about 1 hour). Leave until cold when sides will have contracted from sides of dish. Run a sharp knife around to base. Unmould onto a dish and serve surrounded by picked lettuce leaves. This resembles a cheese when finished and can be cut like a cake.

CACIMPERIO DI TORINO (Cheese and Eggs)

Ingredients:

6 oz. *'Fontina'* cheese (substitute *Gruyère* or *Emmenthal*);	$3\frac{1}{4}$ oz. butter;
a little milk;	4 egg yolks;
	salt and white pepper.

Method: Dice chosen cheese, place in a small bowl, cover with milk and soak for 3 hours. Then place butter in a thick smallish pan, and when butter 'sings' add drained cheese and 2 tablespoons of the soaking milk. Stir over low heat continuously. When cheese has totally dissolved, draw pan from heat and beat in *(fast)* the previously beaten egg yolks. Return to lowest possible heat (ideally over an asbestos mat which is what we always use for cheese fondues). Stir very carefully until mixture becomes like thick cream. Serve with little slices of narrow Italian bread or with bread cubes as for a Swiss Cheese Fondue. In this case the squares or rounds are spread with the *Cacimperio* but you can dip them if preferred.

UOVA ALLA MAIONESE VERDE
(Eggs in Green Mayonnaise)

This is simply an Italian version of Egg Mayonnaise. The eggs are hard boiled for a maximum 10 minutes over strong heat and then they are immersed in cold water. After chilling, eggs are then sliced lengthwise, arranged on a shallow dish and copiously covered with Green Mayonnaise (p. 86).

FRITTATA AL FORMAGGIO
(Italian Cheese Omelette)

This is a flat omelette, not to be confused with the classic French omelette.

Ingredients:

4 standard eggs;

3 generous tablespoons cold water;

1½ oz. grated *Parmesan* cheese; or ¾ oz. each of *Parmesan* and either *Gruyère* or *Emmenthal*;

1 flat teaspoon milled or chopped basil or marjoram (substitute parsley heads);

salt and black pepper to season;

1 oz. butter.

Method: Set omelette pan over a low heat quite dry and allow to become hot. Break eggs into a roomy bowl and beat up lightly with a fork. Then beat in the chosen cheese or cheeses, the chosen herb and a light seasoning of salt and pepper. Toss in butter, raise heat only slightly, and when butter turns browns at edges pour in mixture. Ease sides gently with metal spatula or knife as they begin to set, and once base has set sufficiently (about 2½ minutes) cover with large plate **and cover hand too with tea-cloth lest a drip of hot butter slides out!** Turn pan over. Slide omelette back and just allow to set on opposite side. Serve flat and fast!

MOZZARELLA MILANESE (Cheese and Eggs)

Ingredients:

six ⅛″ thick slices of *Mozzarella* or *Bel Paese* cheese, measuring 4½″ × 2½″;

sifted flour;

2 raw, beaten, strained eggs;

1″ depth of fine, soft white or brown breadcrumbs all in shallow dishes;

deep fryer of hot oil.

Method: Turn chosen cheese slices in flour and dust off surplus. Pass through strained egg and drain off surplus. Bury in the crumbs and pat in carefully. Slide gently into slightly-smoking hot oil and allow to become richly browned all over. Drain on absorbent kitchen paper and serve (optionally) with a light sprinkling of finely chopped parsley overall.

UOVA AL FORMAGGIO (Eggs, Cheese and Ham)

As these are served in individual ramequins or soufflé moulds we give the quantities for 1 only. You can then multiply at will.

Ingredients:

1 egg;

1 very thin, small slice ham;

one $\frac{1}{8}''$ thick circle of *Mozzarella* or *Bel Paese* cheese to fit into base of chosen container;

a little melted butter;

salt and black pepper to season.

Method: Brush the interior of chosen container liberally with melted butter. Lay in ham slice and trim off edges where these rise above the sides. Scissor trimmings finely and scatter over slice. Brush again with melted butter, fit in chosen cheese circle, brush again with melted butter. Break in egg, carefully! Season lightly with salt and pepper. Place on a thick baking sheet and bake in the oven under a light covering of kitchen foil until egg is just set. Gas Mark 4 middle shelf 15/20 minutes.

UOVA CON MAIONESE TONNATA

(Eggs in Tuna Mayonnaise)

Ingredients:

4 soft boiled eggs;

$\frac{1}{2}$ pint tuna mayonnaise (p. 86).

Method: For this delicate and delicious dish the eggs must be shelled soft-boiled. This needs a little care. Lower the eggs on a tablespoon into a fast-boiling water and maintain boiling for exactly 4 minutes, slide instantly into cold water. Tap shells gently all round until completely veined with cracks. Pick one tiny place free of shell with extreme caution. Then hold each egg under a **thin** stream of tap water. This will loosen skin under shell and enable you to peel off remaining shell easily. Lay in chosen, shallow dish, spoon tuna mayonnaise overall.

TORTINI DI POMODORO (Tomato and Eggs)

Ingredients:

1 lb. ripe, skinned tomatoes;

4 eggs;

1 garlic clove;

2 tiny heads fresh mint;

1 oz. butter;

1 fl. oz. olive oil;

1 rounded teaspoon milled parsley;

salt and white pepper;

1½ oz. grated *Parmesan* cheese;

four 3″ square crustless slices of ½″ thick bread;

4 fl. oz. milk;

1 extra, small egg;

hot oil in deep fryer.

Method: Whip extra small egg with milk, pour into soup plate and when oil in fryer throws a slight heat-haze slide bread quickly through egg/milk mixture and lower carefully into hot oil. Fry briskly until brown on both sides, drain on absorbent kitchen paper and keep warm on flat serving dish. Rough-cut tomatoes. Heat oil and melt butter until sizzling in smallish thick pan. Chop mint finely and put with tomatoes, crushed garlic and parsley into oil and butter mixture and simmer gently until tomatoes are pulp. Draw pan away from heat while you whip eggs with a fork, season with salt and pepper and whip in *Parmesan*. Pour onto tomato mixture, stir briskly with sharp-edged spoon until the consistency of creamy scrambled egg. Divide between the *croûtons* and serve fast.

FONDUTA (Italian Cheese 'Fondue')

Incidentally it is important to know that Fondue does not mean cheese. It means a creamy mixture and can be made with a number of vegetables, like Tomato Fondue etc., as well as with cheeses. In Switzerland each canton (county) has its own indigenous one. There are regional variants on *Fontina* so we are merely offering one we trust you will enjoy.

Ingredients:

½ lb. Italian *Fontina* cheese (substitute *Gruyère* or *Emmenthal*);

3 well-beaten eggs;

1 generous pinch salt;

1 oz. butter;

2 generous pinches white pepper,

2½ fl. oz. milk;

twelve ½″ slices from a 'flute' of bread or, in England, three ½″ thick slices from any loaf cut 3″ square.

Method: Slice chosen cheese as thinly as possible and cover with milk. Leave to soak for about 5 hours. Melt butter in thickest possible smallish pan (or fondue pot) and for the finest results place over a low heat on an ordinary asbestos mat. Cook while stirring with a wooden spoon until cheese has dissolved and becomes rather stringy. Pour on eggs, still stirring, add salt and pepper and stir until mixture resembles thick cream. Pour into little individual ramequins. Push crustless toasted bread, cut into little triangles, around inside each pot to form small, encircling walls and serve.

SALSE

(Sauces)

SALSA DI POMIDORO (Tomato Sauce)

Ingredients:

8 skinned, medium, ripe tomatoes;

1 oz. butter and 1 oz. oil;

1 crushed garlic clove;

1 very small raw, grated shallot or small onion;

2 tablespoons thick cream;

1 level eggspoon salt;

1 generous pinch black pepper;

1 level teaspoon of both basil and chives.

Method: Heat butter and oil in a small thick pan. Add tomatoes, garlic and onion and place over a moderate heat. As mixture begins to heat through, press down with the back of a spoon until mixture is pulped and very creamy. Add remaining ingredients. Work down again until thoroughly blended. Sieve and serve.

SALSA GENOVESE (Veal and Vegetables)

Ingredients:

1 medium carrot;

1 fairly large onion;

one 6″ stick white of celery very finely chopped;

4 oz. chopped or coarsely minced veal;

3 medium or 2 large skinned, cored, de-pipped tomatoes;

2 oz. chopped, unskinned mushrooms or 1 oz. dried mushrooms soaked overnight;

8 fl. oz. stock and 5–6 fl. oz. dry white wine or 13–14 fl. oz. stock;

$\frac{3}{4}$ oz. butter;

$\frac{3}{4}$ fl. oz. pure oil;

1 oz. flour;

salt and pepper to season.

Method: Dissolve butter with oil. When hot fry onion gently for 2/3 minutes then add all remaining vegetables, work in and fry for a further 1 minute, then add the veal. Turn and work with wooden spoon and allow mixture to bubble gently until slightly browned. Work in the prepared tomatoes. Turn well and work in the flour. When the mixture becomes pasty, work in the wine gradually (when using) and then the stock, working mixture down until it bubbles after each fluid addition. Taste, correct seasoning with salt and pepper and simmer with an occasional stir for about 25/30 minutes.

RAGU BOLOGNESE (Bologna Sauce)

Ingredients:

8 oz. lean minced beef;

4 oz. chickens' livers;

3 oz. bacon or raw ham;

1 medium carrot;

1 fairly large onion;

one 4″ piece of white celery;

3 rounded teaspoons concentrated tomato *purée*;

1 oz. butter;

1 fl. oz. pure oil;

6 fl. oz. Italian white wine and 6 fl. oz. stock or all stock;

a little nutmeg;

salt and pepper to season.

Method: Soften butter and heat with oil in large frying pan. Fry very gently the diced bacon or ham. After 2 minutes, add diced onion, carrot and celery. When lightly browned work in beef with wooden spoon, then work in scraped chickens' livers and after a further 3 minutes, the tomato *purée*. Then work in wine and stock or all stock gradually. Taste, correct seasoning **lightly** with salt because of bacon or ham, fairly strongly with pepper and finish with a generous pinch of nutmeg. Simmer until all is fairly thick and everything is tender.

Note: It is permissible to add 4 to 5 fl. oz. cream to this mixture for special occasions.

SUGO DI CARNE (Italian Meat Sauce)

Ingredients:

1 medium onion;

½ lb. lean minced beef;

1 medium carrot;

one 4″ piece white of celery;

3 oz. mushrooms with stalks or 1½ oz. dried mushrooms;

3 fl. oz. dry white cooking wine;

1 generous teaspoon tomato *purée*;

approximately ¾ pint strong meat stock;

1 rounded tablespoon flour;

salt and pepper to season;

1 rounded dessertspoon chopped parsley heads;

½ oz. butter;

½ fl. oz. pure oil.

Method: Dice the onion, carrot, celery and chosen mushrooms very finely. In the case of dried mushrooms, soak overnight before using. Heat oil and butter together in large frying pan and when hot fry onion for 1 minute, add carrot, parsley heads, celery and mushrooms and cook gently for 4/5 minutes. Work in the meat with the back of a wooden spoon and let mixture brown slightly all over. Then scatter flour over top surface and work down until mixture is pasty using a wooden spoon. Work in the tomato *purée,* then the wine gradually and finally ½ pint of the stock. Correct seasoning. Simmer, stirring occasionally and, if mixture over-thickens, add more stock to achieve only a fairly thick texture. This is a sauce which can be used with literally any pasta. You can also make a meal out of the Potato *Gnocchi* (p. 69) by sieving this sauce and serving it with them.

SALSA SPINACI (Spinach Sauce)

Ingredients:

1¼ pints thick white sauce;

4 oz. cooked spinach *purée* (p. 68);

2 oz. grated *Parmesan* cheese;

½ oz. butter;

salt and pepper to season.

Method: While basic white sauce is still piping hot, stir in cheese and spinach over heat until cheese has completely dissolved. Correct seasoning with salt and pepper to taste. Stir in a scrap of butter, pour over the *Cannelloni* as explained. If you should dislike spinach, substitute 2 table-spoons Italian Tomato Sauce, *Salsa Pizzaiola,* for spinach.

SALSA DI FUNGHI (Mushroom Sauce)

Ingredients:

2 slices fatty ham diced small or 4 rashers de-rinded diced bacon;

2 oz. butter;

2 oz. olive oil;

1 medium, coarse-grated onion;

1 crushed garlic clove;

1 rounded tablespoon freshly milled parsley heads;

½ lb. unskinned very small mushrooms – 6 oz. sliced and

2 oz. of the smallest left whole;

salt and pepper to season;

1 rounded tablespoon flour;

1 flat teaspoon oregano (wild thyme) or ordinary if you must;

2 tablespoons stock and 2 tablespoons *Marsala,* or 4 tablespoons stock.

Method: Heat oil and the 2 oz. butter together and when sizzling, fry the onion until well-coloured. Place sliced mushrooms in centre of pan and sprinkle the small ones carefully around the outer edges so that you can turn them separately with tongs while, of course, the remainder can be turned with an ordinary metal slice or spatula. Turn and fry for just long enough for mushrooms to achieve a good colour. As soon as the mushrooms have begun to fry add the ham or bacon and continue cooking until all ingredients are lightly browned. Lift out whole mushrooms and set aside. Add crushed garlic, chosen thyme, turn again and then sprinkle flour over the surface. By this time the mushroom juices will have run freely and the flour worked in with the back of a wooden spoon, so will only need the stock or stock and *Marsala* to be added. Correct seasoning with salt and pepper and for high days and holidays be thoroughly reckless and finish with a spoonful or 2 of cream.

SALSA PIZZAIOLA (Neapolitan Tomato Sauce)

This is greatly used in Italian kitchens for spreading on grilled pieces of meat and fish as well as serving with pastas.

Ingredients:

1 lb. skinned, cored, de-pipped fresh tomatoes;

1 fairly large peeled, crushed garlic clove;

3 large-ish fresh basil leaves finely chopped or the same of crushed dried basil;

1 flat teaspoon chopped, fresh oregano (wild thyme) whenever possible, otherwise substitute ordinary thyme;

2 oz. butter or oil;

salt and pepper to season.

Method: Dissolve butter and heat or just heat oil, work in tomato flesh and work down over a very low heat with the back of a wooden spoon. When partly collapsed, work in remaining ingredients. Correct seasoning with salt and pepper and use.

SALSA VERDE (Green Mayonnaise)

Ingredients:

2 separated egg yolks;

½ pint olive oil;

2 dessertspoons wine vinegar;

1 scant flat teaspoon of salt;

1 scant flat coffeespoon of white pepper;

1½ oz. fresh basil leaves (substitute parsley);

1½ oz. pine kernels;

1 dessertspoon lemon juice;

1 flat eggspoon French Mustard (optional).

Method: Place egg yolks, salt, pepper and (optionally a flat eggspoon of French mustard) in a bowl and whip relentlessly until very thick, add oil drip by drip until mayonnaise has 'taken' and begun to thicken. Add oil more copiously and cut as it becomes very thick with wine vinegar, until all oil has been absorbed. Place roughly-chopped basil leaves or picked parsley heads in a mortar with pine kernels and lemon juice and pound relentlessly to a pap. Whip this into mayonnaise.

GARLIC OIL

This is our own, we make it annually. Crush 1 lb. peeled garlic cloves, place in a quart jar, fill up with pure olive oil. Stir regularly once every week for 4 weeks. Leave thereafter indefinitely. Strain off in minute quantities and use as required. REMEMBER IT IS VERY CONCENTRATED. It also saves hours of crushing, a mere teaspoonful is enough for ½ pint of ordinary French Dressing or will flavour ½ pint of basic mayonnaise.

SALSA DI TONNO (Tuna Mayonnaise)

Ingredients:

3 oz. tinned tuna;

1 heaped tablespoon fresh, milled parsley heads;

1 oz. pressed capers;

1 sieved hard-boiled egg yolk;

3 fl. oz. olive oil;

1 raw egg yolk;

the strained juice of ½ medium lemon;

2 generous pinches black pepper.

Method: Place tuna in a mortar and pound down with a pestle until smooth. Add capers, raw egg yolk, sieved hard-boiled egg yolk and parsley and pound again until perfectly smooth. Pound in oil very gradually and when once again smooth pound in lemon juice and pepper.

Note: The tuna oil may be used instead of given olive oil and merely made up to given quantity with olive oil. You choose!

SALSA CALDA (Hot Tomato Sauce)

Ingredients:

½ pint bone stock;

1 rounded teaspoon Indian Curry Paste (Masala);

1 rounded teaspoon salt;

1 domed eggspoon pepper;

1 rounded dessertspoon soft brown (pieces) sugar;

½ lb. skinless tomato pulp from tin or home bottled.

Method: Place all ingredients in a small pan and stir until mixture comes to the boil. Steady off the heat to a steady simmer and maintain for 10/12 minutes to reduce pan contents. Sieve sauce, stir and send to table in a sauce boat.

SALSA AGRODOLCE (Modern Sweet-Sour Sauce)

Ingredients:

2 oz. castor sugar;

1 fl. oz. water;

2 fl. oz. wine vinegar;

1 flat tablespoon pine kernels;

thinnest possible peel from 1 small orange.

Method: Place sugar and water in a small thick pan and allow to dissolve and turn strong golden colour. Meanwhile turn peel over to pith side and cut away all remaining until the pock marks of the peel show clearly all over. Then cut into hair-thin strips. Place in another small pan, cover liberally with cold water, bring to the boil, strain, return to pan, re-cover with water and repeat altogether 3 times. When finally strained strips are ready to use and shorn of all bitterness. When sugar has become syrupy and golden brown stir in vinegar off the heat, return to mere thread of heat and stir, adding pine kernels, for 3 to a maximum 4 minutes. Cool, pour over eggs and serve lightly seasoned with salt and pepper.

PEPERONATA (Pimento Sauce)

Ingredients:

5 peeled red pimentoes;

1 lb. ripe tomatoes;

6 oz. finely sliced onions;

2 oz. butter;

2 fl. oz. oil or 4 fl. oz. oil and omit butter;

salt and pepper to season.

Method: Halve (top to bottom) pimentoes. Remove every scrap of pith and all pips. Place cut side downwards on grill and grill under moderate heat until skins crack and blister. Then peel (easily!). Salt and pepper.

Skin, de-seed and remove tomato cores. Heat oil and butter or just oil in a thick pan. Reduce heat to low and soft fry onions until almost tender. Add pimentoes, cut into strips. Cover and simmer until tender. Add tomatoes and cook on for further 10 minutes. Season and use.

Note 1: Garlic is purely optional but we think it adds greatly to the flavour of this mixture.

Note 2: When using as a sauce, rub through a sieve.

BAGNA CAUDA (Pungent Italian Dipping Sauce)

This mixture can be made well in advance and our means of discovering this fact were slightly unorthodox. A batch was made and put into a lidded fondue pot and put on a top shelf in our kitchen, out of everyone's way. The day of the terrace party, it poured with rain, the *Bagna Cauda* was forgotten and was discovered 3 months later, still in excellent condition!

Ingredients:

½ pint Spanish olive oil;

6 cloves garlic;

4 oz. anchovy fillets;

pinch of saffron;

½ eggspoon milled black peppercorns.

Method: Warm the oil in a small, thick pan. Fling in the **sliced** garlic cloves, the seasonings and chopped anchovies. When the brew bubbles, gather your guests around to dunk salad segments in the sauce set over a spirit stove.

Dunking Items: Raw sliced cabbage, raw ribbon-cut pimentoes, celery, spring onions, chicory leaves, chips of raw carrot, cardoons, etc.

INSALATA

(Salads)

INSALATA DI PEPERONI . No. 1

(Pimentoes and tomatoes)

Ingredients:

2 green pimentoes weighing 11 oz.;

1¼ lb. ripe tomatoes;

1 generous pinch salt;

2 generous pinches black pepper;

4 fl. oz. olive oil;

1 tablespoon wine vinegar;

1 heaped teaspoon finely scissored chives;

1 heaped teaspoon milled fresh parsley heads.

Method: Halve pimentoes lengthwise, remove all white pith and pips. Cut into thin strips lengthwise. Slice unskinned tomatoes thinly, mix well together and arrange on chosen dish. Sprinkle with salt and pepper. Pour oil overall, sprinkle with little drops of wine vinegar and scatter overall with chives and parsley. This is one of the simplest salads suitable for any cold meat, game or poultry.

INSALATA DI RICOTTA E FUNGHI

(Raw Mushrooms, Cream Cheese)

Ingredients for each portion:

2–3 oz. *Ricotta* or home made cream cheese;

1 flat dessertspoon freshly milled parsley heads;

3–4 thinly sliced unskinned mushrooms, quantity will depend on size;

Salsa Verde (p. 86);

1 pinch of milled black peppercorns;

1 pinch of celery salt.

Method: Pipe a fat rosette of chosen cheese with a No. 7 pipe in a nylon icing bag into the centre of chosen platter or dish. Surround with a narrow border of parsley and sprinkle a little parsley, salt and pepper over the cheese. Place a double row of mushroom slices to form a flower-like circle. Cover mushrooms liberally with *Salsa Verde*.

IL CAPPONE IN GALLERIA

(Anchovies, Olives, Capers)

Ingredients:

6 neatly trimmed new-bread crusts;

12 anchovy fillets in oil;

1 oz. green olives;

2 rounded dessertspoons pressed capers;

1 good sized peeled, crushed garlic clove;

olive oil and wine vinegar.

Method: If using a 'flute' or 'baton' of Continental bread, instead of English loaf-crusts, which we recommend whenever possible, cut 3 lengths of 4″, split in halves, remove all but the inside crumb against crust walls, so that you obtain 6 shallow troughs, and spread with the crushed garlic, rubbing it in thoroughly as for garlic crust/matchsticks in a classic French Potato Salad. Drip oil very gently over to moisten, using only sufficient for the crusts to absorb. Then, in $\frac{1}{4}$ proportion to the oil used, drip wine vinegar over the crusts to complete the moistening; but for pity's sake do not make them soggy! Chop the capers, and spread lightly over prepared crusts. Peel olives off their stones, just like peeling an apple so that each one becomes a fleshy coil. Lay an anchovy fillet down centre, set coil of olive flesh on top and brush overall with a little more oil. Finally sprinkle (optionally) with black pepper. Otherwise follow the recipe using ordinary English bread crusts.

Note: This 'salad' is as prodigious a thirst-promoter at drinks parties as *Bagna Cauda* (p. 94).

INSALATA D'INDIVIA (Chicory)

Indivia is yet one more name to add to the totally confusing collection used by the common market countries. While *indivia* is the Italian for chicory, in France chicory is *endive,* the name the English give with merely a difference in pronunciation to what the French call 'Chicoree'. The Belgians add to the confusion by calling chicory *'whitloof'* and so on. . . . This is not a recipe so much as a description. The chicory, sold or grown **blanched,** with tightly packed leaves, is very prone to blackening. So first **pull** off the leaves, right down to the final tiny little core. Set this aside. Optionally tear leaves in 2 if 'heads' are large thus yielding rather big leaves. NEVER CUT ANY MEMBER OF THE GREEN SALAD FAMILY and chicory IS green though blanched before eating, like dandelion leaves. Then toss in a wooden bowl with equal quantities of strained lemon juice and water. Leave 30 minutes. Drain and work approximately $\frac{1}{4}$ a medium-sized garlic clove to pulp by pressing it down with the tip of an ordinary, small table knife. Work this amount, with 2 chopped mint leaves in the same manner to achieve a paste, place in a small bowl and work in oil gradually with a seasoning of salt and pepper to taste. Turn over chicory and garnish with sprigs of mint.

Note: In season, peeled, fresh quartered walnuts add greatly to the character of this simple salad.

INSALATA DI FUNGHI GENOVESE
(Raw Mushrooms)

This is without any doubt one of the very best ways of eating mushrooms. If you have never tried it, please do, at the earliest opportunity.

Ingredients:

$\frac{1}{2}$ lb. raw, white button or cup mushrooms;	salt;
6 anchovy fillets;	1 dessertspoon strained lemon juice;
2 fl. oz. olive oil;	$\frac{1}{2}$ small, crushed garlic clove.

Method: Place un-skinned mushrooms in a sieve,* pour a quart of boiling water slowly over them to clean and scald. Wipe dry in a cloth, slice thinly, with stalks, toss into a salad bowl. Work up oil, garlic, and lemon juice, swill overall, turn well with a couple of wooden spoons and only add salt at the moment of service if omitting anchovies. Turn onto a shallow dish, trellis with well-wiped anchovy fillets and serve under a light, optional dusting of fresh milled parsley heads.

*All the best of mushrooms' flavours lies in and just under the skin, by this treatment hygiene is served and the best of flavour retained.

INSALATA DI PEPERONI. No. 2

(Pimentoes, Celery, Tomatoes)

Ingredients:

3 large, ideally yellow
pimentoes;

6 firm, small tomatoes;

1 crushed garlic clove;

1 dozen small hard, round
radishes (red);

1 small heart of white celery;

oil and wine vinegar.

Method: Halve pimentoes, remove all pith and pips and slice very thinly, unskinned. Slice unskinned tomatoes thinly, toss both into a salad bowl with the celery heart and radishes also sliced thinly. Moisten with drips of oil until shiny but not soaked. Add a few drops of wine vinegar, toss again and scatter on the crushed garlic turning until well distributed.

INSALATA DI PATATE CON TONNO

(Potato and Tuna Salad)

Ingredients:

one 4/5 oz. tin tuna in oil;

1 lb. new or old potatoes;

1 rounded teaspoon pressed capers;

salt;

black pepper;

1 large firm onion;

2 fl. oz. olive oil;

1 fl. oz. wine vinegar;

1 rounded dessertspoon fresh,
milled parsley.

Method: Scrub and steam chosen potatoes. Skin, slice and season carefully with salt and black pepper. Peel and slice onion as thinly as possible. Separate onion rings. Toss into bowl with potatoes and mix. Turn vinegar and oil overall and turn very thoroughly. Arrange in serving bowl, dot with small cubes of tuna, pour own oil over and sprinkle with parsley and capers. Serve straight away.

INSALATA DI FAGIOLI (White Bean Salad)

The white beans, the best of which come from Tuscany, are not easily obtainable in England, so settle for haricot or butter beans. We have met this salad in concert with a T. Bone Steak in Florence, as an hors d'oeuvre *(antipasto)* in Milan, Rome, Brindisi and points between. The 2 best known treatments are with onions and with tuna.

Ingredients:

½ lb. haricot or butter beans;

cold water;

salt and white pepper;

1 large onion;

¼ pint olive oil;

one 4/5 oz. tin tuna (optional);

1 lemon.

Method: Place beans to soak in cold water, making sure that water comes at least 1″ above beans to allow for expansion. Leave for a minimum 12 hours. Drain, cover with fresh, cold water, and bring to the boil. Level off thereafter at a steady simmer and maintain until beans are **not** *al dente*! – but tender. Refresh in cold water. Season with salt and white pepper. Turn into a salad bowl, turn and turn again with the olive oil and the peeled onion cut very thinly and then each round halved and separated. Add lemon juice. When very thoroughly impregnated leave in mild refrigeration for at least 2 hours. Just before service put the (optional) tuna, in small cubes over the top surface and pour on the tuna oil too.

Note: We regard the tuna as essential when serving this salad with fish or vegetable assemblies but not when serving with meats.

CAPPON MAGRO DI LIGURIA
(Mixed Vegetables)

This is a charming presentation when wishing to show off a little. The main, ordinary vegetables are built into a pyramid, a sauce is then poured overall and wooden (never plastic) cocktail sticks or miniature skewers are threaded with tit-bits and driven in at the moment of (well chilled) service. Ingredients are subject to many variations.

Suggested Typical Ingredients:

1 small cauliflower;	½ lb. potatoes;
¼ lb. French beans;	1 doz. shrimps or 3/4 small scollops;
¼ lb. baby broad beans;	6 large, stoned olives;*
¼ lb. young carrots;	2 hard boiled eggs;
¼ lb. celery heart;	½ crushed garlic clove.

Method: Steam carrots, un-peeled new potatoes, French beans, young peas, the flower of cauliflower, broad beans and French beans. Divide cauliflower into sprigs, cut potatoes into cubes, and dice French beans, carrots, raw celery, and mix potatoes with just enough oil and wine vinegar dressing to bind. Shape into a small pyramid on a platter well rubbed with the crushed garlic. Now press a tapering line, of ½ the carrots, from top carrots to bottom. And so continue all round the pyramid with all diced vegetables baby broad beans and peas. Quarter celery head and drive 4 quarters at outwards slanting angles into tip of pyramid. Pour special sauce overall. Drive 1 prawn, 1 stoned olive, and 1 piece of cooked scollop with a ⅛″ slice of lengthwise-cut hard boiled egg onto each skewer or cocktail stick. Spike these decoratively into pyramid and serve.

The special sauce.

3 washed wiped anchovy fillets from brine; 1 tablespoon fresh milled parsley heads, 2 spikes of tarragon (2″ long) also milled, 1 dessertspoon pressed capers, 4 fl. oz. olive oil, black pepper and 1 tablespoon strained lemon juice. Pound fillets with parsley, tarragon and capers. When reduced to a mere pulp, beat in olive oil very gradually to obtain a sauce consistency. Cut in lemon juice, beat again, add black pepper to taste.

*To our knowledge the Americans are the only importers of fat, green, stoned (they call them pitted) olives. As stockists are most variable a telephone to the Trade Section of the American Embassy will be the best source of up to date, reliable information. These are also ideal for the *Antipasto Olive Ripiene* (p. 17).

BAGNA CAUDA (Pungent Dip)

Assorted salad vegetables and a pungent sauce dip. Although, strictly speaking, this is a drinks party assembly which promotes thirst prodigiously, it belongs in this salad section because it is entirely composed of salad items save for the sauce (p. 88).

Ingredients: These are immensely variable according to the season. They can and do include, trimmed spring onions, sticks of heart of celery, 'fingers' of un-skinned cucumber, strips of de-pipped and pithed red/ yellow/green pimentoes, trimmed radishes, fingers of cooked beetroot and red of carrot (not the yellowy cores please), raw globe artichoke leaves (they blacken the teeth!), separated, blanched chicory (English) leaves, florets of raw, small cauliflowers (large ones are too coarse!), slices of scalded un-skinned mushrooms with their trimmed stems, the leaves of cos lettuce heart, picked sprigs of endive, and many more. The presentation is both easy and most attractive. Take any large flat platter, set the Bagna Cauda Sauce (p. 88) in the centre, heap your chosen assortment in decorative piles and set on a small table. Then everyone can pick and dunk at will.

Note: Classically the cardoon is a must in Italy, but this is little used in England and may prove impossible to find, unless you grow it yourselves; but still you should be made aware of this fact in an Italian Cookery book!

DOLCI E GELATI

(Puddings and Ice Cream)

ZABAIONE (Famous Italian Custard)

In recent years, we have completely by-passed the old domestic trick of making this famous, easy dish over an outer pan of hot water. If you follow our method exactly you will achieve a golden velvet foam every single time.

Ingredients:

4 egg yolks;

four $\frac{1}{2}$ egg shells of *Marsala* (no substitute for this);

2 dessertspoons cold water;

4 heaped teaspoons castor sugar.

Method: Place wine and water in a thick pan. Whip egg yolks and sugar together thoroughly. Scrape mixture onto warmed wine and water and whip relentlessly, putting pan on a medium heat, off for an instant and on and off again until mixture rises up the pan and becomes like golden velvet. Stop whipping and test (off the heat). If runny whip on again until mixture just flops idly off a lifted spoon. Turn into glasses and serve at blood heat.

SPUMONI ZABAIONE (Marsala Ice Cream)

To make the absolutely delectable Marsala Ice Cream of this name you follow the recipe as for *Zabaione* (above), but you also set ready a large bowl half-filled with crushed ice and $\frac{1}{4}$ pint fairly stiffly whipped double cream. Then when the *Zabaione* is like golden velvet you plunge the panful into the ice and whip on steadily until the mixture descends to blood heat. Then spoon on the prepared cream still whipping until all is incorporated and simply freeze.

ZABAIONE CON PESCHE (with Peaches)

Ingredients:

1 given batch *Zabaione* (p. 95);   4 oz. almond paste;

4 small peaches;   a little sifted icing sugar.

Method: Peel and halve peaches and remove the stones. Make almond paste into 4 balls of the size of the peach stones. Clap the peach halves over these. Set on a baking sheet, dust liberally with sifted icing sugar and slip into the oven at Gas Mark 4, 1 shelf above centre, while you make the *Zabaione*. Place a peach in each of 4 glasses, pour the *Zabaione* equally overall and serve.

FIOR DI LOTO (Meringue with Zabaione)

This is a great delicacy.

Ingredients:

5 not-too-fresh, separated egg whites;   1 batch made but not frozen *Spumoni Zabaione* (p. 95);

2 oz. and a separate 6 oz. castor sugar;   a little olive oil.

Method: Cut a sheet of greaseproof paper to fit a baking sheet which will contain a 9″ diameter circle of meringue. Draw a 9″ circle on the greaseproof. Turn over and brush very thoroughly indeed with oil until paper is thoroughly impregnated. Lay, oiled side uppermost, on baking sheet. Whip eggs until just stiff. Sprinkle given 2 oz. sugar over and continue whipping for exactly 3 minutes with electric mixer. Allow 5 minutes for rotary hand whisk. Stop beating, clean off beaters of all meringue and cut remaining sugar in gently with a plastic spatula. Spread mixture to a depth of generous $\frac{1}{4}$″ over entire circle. Then place just over $\frac{1}{3}$ of remaining meringue in a nylon icing bag* with a No. 7 metal crown pipe affixed. Then pipe a fat border around so that outside edge of it comes to extreme edge of spread meringue base. Dry out in the oven at Gas Mark 2 for 30 minutes on 1 shelf below centre. Take out and while still hot, pipe a slightly narrower border over the one which is now set. This merely means that you exert a little less pressure on bag and pull pipe round a shade thinner. Return to oven, same temperature and position for a further 30 minutes. Repeat piping a third time return to oven exactly as before – the completed case therefore has an overall 1 hour 30 minutes baking. Cool case. Remove onto serving dish and make *Spumoni Zabaione* mixture; but do not fill into case until just before serving. Roll out the almond paste and cut into an $8\frac{1}{2}$″ circle. Lower this gently into cold meringue case. Then store in aluminium foil in a plastic, air-tight lidded

*Obtainable from L. Jaeggi & Son, Tottenham Court Road, London W.1.

box and keep in a cool place until required. For service, just turn *Spumoni* mixture over almond paste. In season, decorate the meringue sides with pairs of un-stalked, stoned cherries stuffed with scraps of the almond paste and hang them over the rims. Out of season, sink in the skinless segments of 2 oranges or skinless peach or in their season immerse hulled, cut strawberries.

Almond Paste (with Marsala)

Work up 4 oz. sifted icing sugar with 2 oz. ground almonds, 1 tablespoon Marsala and a few drops of raw, unbeaten egg white. Roll out to a generous $\frac{1}{4}''$ diameter and cut into an $8\frac{1}{2}''$ diameter circle.

BOMBERINI (Super Doughnuts)

An enchanting and very stout old dame hawks these in a gingham covered basket along the sands at Viareggio. She gets up at 4 a.m., makes a basket full and sells them to holiday makers, thereby ensuring total ruination of waistlines!

Ingredients:

$\frac{1}{2}$ oz. fresh yeast;	grated rind of $\frac{1}{4}$ lemon;
$2\frac{1}{2}$ fl. oz. warm milk;	apricot jam;
$\frac{1}{4}$ oz. castor sugar;	$\frac{1}{4}$ pint warm milk;
2 oz. flour;	2 oz. sugar;
6 egg yolks;	extra flour for kneading;
3 oz. softened butter;	raw egg white for sealing;
1 tablespoon rum;	castor sugar.
10 oz. flour;	

Method: To make yeast ferment dissolve yeast and $\frac{1}{4}$ oz. sugar in $2\frac{1}{2}$ fl. oz. warm milk, stir in the 2 oz. flour, carefully removing all lumps. Leave in warm place, covered, to ferment. Whisk egg yolks and 2 oz. sugar in a bowl over hot water until light, beat in softened butter, rum and lemon rind. When yeast fermentation has subsided, add egg mixture and the $\frac{1}{4}$ pint warm milk. Stir in flour. Leave to rise in a warm place, covered, until doubled in size. When risen, knock back and turn onto a floured surface. Knead until smooth, throwing it between your hands on the surface incorporating enough flour to make a workable dough. Roll out dough on a floured board to $\frac{1}{3}''$ thick. Cut out oblongs $4'' \times 3''$. Spread 1 heaped teaspoon apricot jam along the length of the cut out oblong. Roll up and seal edges with raw egg white. Place on a floured cloth and cover. Leave to prove for about 30 minutes. Fry in deep fat, slightly under smoking point until golden brown. While still hot turn in castor sugar.

PIZZA ARANCI (Orange)

Ingredients:

1 lb. bread dough;	apricot glaze;
½ pint milk;	2 oz. castor sugar;
4 small oranges;	1 teaspoon rennet;
1½ oz. flaked almonds;	1 flat dessertspoon castor sugar.

Method: Roll out dough to a 10″ diameter circle, i.e. the size of a large dinner plate. Pinch the edges of dough between thumb and first finger or with a pair of pastry cook's pinchers and lay it on a buttered and floured baking sheet. Warm milk to blood heat. Stir in rennet and dessertspoon castor sugar. Leave until set. Cut the surface of the made junket with a spoon, place in a piece of muslin, drain off any surplus whey and spread the curds quite thickly over the raw dough surface. Cut pith and peel off oranges simultaneously. Cut up orange slices and lay over the pizza surface. Sprinkle with the flaked almonds. Dust with the castor sugar and bake at Gas Mark 5, middle shelf, for 20/23 minutes. While still hot brush top with apricot glaze and serve hot. If wishing to serve cold, make with bought or home-made puff paste instead of bread dough.

Apricot Glaze

Ingredients:

½ lb. apricot jam;	2 tablespoons sweet white wine or water.

Method: Rub jam through a sieve into a small pan. Add chosen fluid and heat and stir until smooth. Paint over item with a pastry brush.

PIZZA DI FRUTTA (Pineapple)

Ingredients:

½ lb. bought or home-made puff paste;	4 home-bottled black cherries or tinned cherries or glacé cherries;
approximately 6 oz. sieved apricot jam;	a little egg wash.
5 whole pineapple rings, fresh or tinned, and 2 extra quartered ones;	

Method: Roll out paste to a 9¾″ diameter circle, ¼″ in depth. Lay on a lightly floured baking sheet, not on a wetted one because we do not want this to rise too much. Then nick all round edge in little ½″ doorsteps. Brush all over with egg wash. Place in the oven, Gas Mark 6, one shelf above centre and bake to a fairly strong golden brown. Cool on a rack, flatten down any risen pastry and brush all over with approximately $\frac{1}{2}$ the sieved jam. Cover this surface with the 5 pineapple rings and fill the interstices with the quartered pieces. Cover with remaining jam *purée,* sink in chosen cherries and, if liked, finish with a sprig or two of angelica.

Note: This may also be made with bread dough if preferred.

SPECIAL CREAM CHEESE

(Substitute for Italian types)

Ingredients:

1 pint gradually assembled top-of-the-milk from gold label bottles;

$\frac{1}{2}$ pint single or coffee cream;

$\frac{1}{2}$ pint double cream;

2 dessertspoons rennet.

Method: Heat milk and cream in a large saucepan over a mere thread of heat until really hot. When mixture is blood heat, turn into roomy bowl and add the rennet. Allow to set in a cool place but do not refrigerate. When set line out an ordinary sieve with a double fold of butter muslin. Spoon in the now set rennet/milk and cream mixture. Knot the 4 ends of the muslin securely together while this is still in the sieve. Hang up muslin bag and allow to drip for 48 hours, by which time it will have ceased dripping but the cream cheese will still not be quite firm enough. Complete the job by hanging muslin-bagged cheese in a draught for a further 24 hours.

CROSTATA DI RICOTTA

(Flan with Cheese, Grapes and Pine Kernels)

Ingredients:

1 raw, sweet short paste flan case;

1 lb. *Ricotta* cheese or home-made cream cheese Versions 1 or 2 (above and p. 101);

$3\frac{3}{4}$ oz. castor sugar;

1 rounded tablespoon flour;

1 generous pinch salt;

1 rounded tablespoon finely grated orange rind;

4 separated egg yolks;

1 egg white, unbeaten;

2 oz. peeled, de-pipped white grapes;

2 rounded tablespoons mixed, candied peel;

2 rounded tablespoons blanched, flaked almonds or whole pine nuts;

a little sifted icing sugar.

Method: Place chosen cheese in roomy bowl with sugar, flour, salt, orange rind and egg yolks. Blend very thoroughly together. Add grapes and candied peel and work these in thoroughly. Spread into raw sweet short paste case. Smooth off top surface evenly and spread with raw unbeaten egg white. Then sprinkle with chosen nuts, sprinkle lightly with sifted icing sugar and trellis with trimmings of sweet short paste left over from the flan case. Bake on middle shelf of oven at Gas Mark 4 for between 45 and 60 minutes, i.e. until the mixture is firm and the cooked paste is a light golden brown on both top and sides.

CREMA DI MASCHERPONE
(Cold Cream Cheese Pudding)

The original of this is an unsalted cream cheese made from thick cream which is called *Mascherpone* and is generally found in the Lombardy area of Italy. As we have done, you can replace this with home-made cream cheese.

Ingredients:

½ batch home-made cream cheese, preferably Version 2 (p. 101);

2 oz. sifted icing sugar;

2 separated egg yolks;

1–1½ tablespoons kirsch (from a miniature bottle);

1 given batch of egg yolk sponge;

the strained juice of 1 small orange;

a little *Crème Chantilly*.

Method: Make and bake sponge (see below), place in chosen dish and moisten with the orange juice. Beat up the egg yolks with the sugar, add the kirsch and beat again. Beat this mixture – when absolutely smooth – into the cream cheese. Turn into a small oiled mould and either freeze for 2–3 hours or stand mould in a larger bowl, surround very liberally with ice cubes and refrigerate overnight. At the moment of service turn out over sponge base and mask the edges of the sponge with a little *Crème Chantilly*.

Egg Yolk Sponge

Ingredients:

3½ oz. castor sugar;
3½ oz. sifted flour;

4 separated egg yolks.

Method: Whip egg yolks alone very thoroughly indeed and then even more thoroughly whip in sugar until mixture is thick, pale and frothy. Then stop whipping altogether and fold in the flour lightly but very thoroughly. Turn into a greaseproof paper-lined, buttered and floured, standard 9″ diameter victoria sponge tin and bake at Gas Mark 4, 1 shelf above centre, for 20 minutes. Invert on a cooling rack and allow to cool before using.

GELATO DI RICOTTA (Gâteau with Cream Cheese)

Ingredients:

7 oz. Italian *Ricotta* cheese (or home-made cream cheese);

5 oz. castor sugar;

2 tablespoons *Crème de Cacao* (from a miniature bottle);

1 pinch vanilla powder (not essence);

2 rounded tablespoons chocolate chips;

2 rounded tablespoons mixed chopped glacé fruits (angelica, cherries, sultanas);

1 Swiss roll sponge panel (p. 102).

Method: Place cheese, sugar, *Cacao* and **real** vanilla in a roomy bowl. Whip until smooth and creamy. Fold in chocolate chips and fruit. Line base and sides of a 6″ diameter × 1½″ deep slope-sided, round tin with sponge, press in cheese mixture, cover with a sponge 'lid'. Cover tightly with foil and freeze either in freezing compartment of refrigerator or in freezer. Dust thickly with sifted icing sugar top and sides just before serving.

SUBSTITUTE CREAM CHEESE

For the home-made cream cheese you will need 2 pints of fresh milk and 1 teaspoon of not too ancient rennet! This tends to lose its capacity to set when it has stood about on a store shelf for months. Warm a roomy bowl, stand on top of your cooker when the oven is in use, pour in milk and stir in the rennet. Leave for 1 hour. Remove and leave until set. Then spoon the mixture into a double fold of muslin laid inside a sieve. Tie the 4 ends together and hang up overnight. When fully dripped and thickly creamy in texture use as explained, for stuffing *Pere Ripiene*.

With any left-overs, work in chopped chives, salt, pepper, 1 or 2 finely chopped black olives, a finely chopped, small gherkin and a teaspoon of powdered paprika to every ¼ lb. Mix well together, chill in refrigeration and serve with bread and butter or with biscuits.

ZUPPA INGLESE (Italian Trifle)

Ingredients:

1 standard Swiss roll sponge panel;

sieved apricot jam;

$\frac{1}{4}$ of a standard batch confectioners' custard;

1 standard batch Swiss meringue mixture;

Strega (Italian liqueur) or apricot brandy from a miniature bottle;

approximately $\frac{1}{4}$ pint sweet white wine.

Method: Divide sponge into 3 equal panels. Mix given wine with *Strega* or brandy from miniature bottle, but do be sparing, *Strega* is strong and crude. Shake $\frac{1}{3}$ over first panel, then spread with confectioners' custard and jam. Repeat with second layer, cover with third layer, and moisten with remaining $\frac{1}{3}$. Then either fork raw meringue mixture all over top and sides till sponge is completely hidden, or spread thinly all over, put remaining meringue mixture into a nylon icing bag with No. 7 Crown pipe and pipe on ornamental scrolls. Dry out to pale biscuit colour in oven, 1 shelf below centre, Gas Mark $\frac{1}{2}$, for approximately 40–50 minutes.

Basic Swiss Roll

Put 3 standard eggs in a bowl for whipping, cover small heat-resistant plate with aluminium foil. Place 4 oz. castor sugar on foil, bake, Gas Mark 7 for 6 minutes, 1 shelf above middle. Impact hot sugar on eggs and whip immediately until almost double in bulk and very foamy. Stop whipping fold in 2$\frac{1}{2}$ oz. sifted flour, spread evenly over $14'' \times 10'' \times \frac{3}{4}''$ standard Swiss roll tin. Lined with fitted base of greaseproof paper well brushed with oil. Bake, Gas Mark 7, 8 to 9 minutes until like golden feathered bed. Turn onto lightly floured, NOT SUGARED, greaseproof paper until covered. Brush off surplus flour.

MERINGHE PANNA MONTATA

(Meringue, Fruit and Cream)

This is nothing more or less than an Italian type of French *Vacherin Chantilly*. As such the meringue case can be filled with any good mousse mixture – not left inside long enough before service for the case to become soggy! Use chocolate, lemon or orange mousse, or a mixture of fruits and ice cream, all surmounted with decorated, piped spirals of whipped cream. Work with our mistake-proof Swiss meringue mixture on page 96. A given 5 egg white batch will be sufficient if your case measures 6'' in diameter but if requiring a 9'' diameter case you will need 1 given batch plus an additional $\frac{1}{2}$ batch. When wishing to make meringue up in 1 batch, whatever the quantity, this can be used for the base and first piped border, refrigerated, and used again for the remaining 2 over-topping piped edge bands. Just follow the instructions given on page 96 for *Fior di Loto* meringue case.

A Typical Italian Assembly

Ingredients:

1–1½ pints *pistachio* ice cream (p. 104);

1 lb. poached, drained fresh figs or one 2 lb. tin figs in syrup likewise drained before use;

½ pint double cream;

1 oz. sifted icing sugar;

1 stiffly whipped egg white.

Method: Have cream ready for last minute assembly and refrigerate when prepared. To prepare, whip cream until it just hangs from whisk. Whip in sugar until stiff. Cut in egg white with a plastic spatula and then blend carefully. When ready to serve pack ice cream in curls (hot-water dipped tablespoon) into meringue case. Quarter and arrange chosen figs over the ice cream. Surmount with *Chantilly* cream which in this case **could** be classically correct if flavoured with *Strega* but go easy with this incredibly strong liqueur!

PERE RIPIENE (Stuffed Pears)

Ingredients:

4 oz. cream cheese;

4 dessert pears;

4 'stalks' of softened angelica;

2 oz. milled pine kernels;

the strained juice of ½ a medium lemon and an equal quantity of cold water.

Method: Mix lemon juice and water. Core the pears unskinned – it is easier as they are not so slippery and there is less fear of bruising them. Use an apple corer at the opposite end to the stems and hollow out as far as possible. Then excavate the stalk end with a pointed, small knife. Place pears together in a small bowl, pour the lemon/water mixture over them and turn occasionally for an overall 30 minutes. Remove. Place cream cheese in a nylon icing bag with a ¼″ writing pipe affixed. With this pipe the cream cheese into the prepared pears. Turn each pear in milled kernels until thoroughly coated. Stand each upon its base end on a small glass plate or dish. Drive in an angelica 'stem'. Chill and serve.

GELATO DI ALBICOCCHE (Apricot Ice Cream)

Ingredients:

4 egg yolks;

½ pint double or whipping cream;

2 lb. tinned, drained, wiped, sieved apricot halves;

one 1″ wide paper-thin strip of lemon peel;

2 oz. sifted icing sugar.

Method: Mix cream with egg yolks, add lemon peel and set over an extremely gentle heat. Begin whipping immediately and continue until mixture becomes thick. Whip in the sugar, remove from the heat, whip down to blood heat, whip in the prepared apricot *purée* then turn into chosen container and freeze.

Alternative treatment: Jettison the tinned apricots given above and replace with dried apricots. These should be soaked in strained cold tea overnight, and then poached with extreme gentleness without sugar until absolutely soft. Strain, sieve the fruit and add as above to the basic, sweetened cream mixture, using 6 oz. sifted icing sugar as against 2 oz. with the tinned apricots.

GELATO DI PISTACCHIO (Pistachio Ice Cream)

Ingredients:

8 fl. oz. single or coffee cream;

4 separated egg yolks;

3 oz. sifted icing sugar;

1½ oz. shelled, milled pistachio nuts;

4 fl. oz. double or whipping cream;

a few drops of green vegetable colouring;

2 oz. ground almonds;

2 oz. chopped pistachio nuts.

Method: Place single cream in a small, thick pan. Bring to the boil over a low heat. Meanwhile place egg yolks and given sugar in a bowl and whip until this is pale golden and foamy. Pour hot cream on gradually whipping all the time and until thoroughly blended. Whip in the milled nuts, return mixture to pan and stir constantly over low heat until mixture coats the back of a lifted wooden spoon. Stir in the double or whipping cream and vegetable colouring, strain and finally fold in ground almonds and chopped nuts. Freeze.

DOLCE TORINESE (Chocolate)

Swiftly made, easy, can be frozen extremely successfully.

Ingredients:

8 oz. softened chocolate chips;

4 fl. oz. rum;

½ lb. butter (preferably unsalted);

2 oz. sifted icing sugar;

2 separated eggs;

5 oz. grated, finely chopped pine kernels;

12 *petit beurre* biscuits;

cream and icing sugar for garnish.

Method: Cream butter until very pale and loose and fluffy. Beat in icing sugar and egg yolks singly, whipping steadily. Soften chocolate over hot water, beat well, add rum, cool down a little and meanwhile add pine kernels to butter mixture, then cooled chocolate mixture. Fold in biscuits cut into $1'' \times \frac{1}{2}''$ pieces, turn into a buttered bun tin measuring $7\frac{3}{4}'' \times 4'' \times 2\frac{1}{4}''$. Chill or freeze. Unmould for service, top with whipped cream and dust liberally with sifted icing sugar.

CASSATA SICILIANA (Sicilian *Gâteau*)

Very special and a great success as either a pudding or a *gâteau*.

Ingredients:

1 small pound cake;

1 tablespoon double cream;

½ lb. *Ricotta* cheese (substitute home-made cream cheese);

a generous 1½ oz. sifted icing sugar;

1 fl. oz. *Strega* (very powerful!) or 2 tablespoons *Orange Curaçao* (better but not classically correct);

2 oz. chopped glacé cherries;

½ oz. chopped angelica;

½ oz. chopped, mixed peel;

1 oz. coarsely chopped plain (sweet-shop) chocolate;

6 oz. chocolate chips;

2½ fl. oz. very strong black coffee;

4 oz. unsalted butter.

Method: Trim the cake free of its outer top, base and all sides. Slice the remainder lengthwise into ½″ slices. If choosing *Ricotta* rub through sieve before starting work, if using cream cheese this is unnecessary. Then place in an electric mixer bowl and whip fast, whipping in gradually the cream, sugar and chosen liqueur. Stop whipping. Fold in fruit, plain chocolate, angelica and peel, and use, evenly spread, over base layer of cake, building up the shape with remaining layers all spread thickly with mixture so as to use all you have made and are left with a single 'lid' layer un-spread.

Cover overall with this. Chill in refrigeration until very firm, or put for shorter time in freezer to firm up. Meanwhile make the chocolate icing. Place the chocolate chips and coffee in a small, thick pan and dissolve very slowly, then beat until absolutely smooth. Then chop the butter into small dice and while chocolate mixture is still piping hot whip in gradually, whipping all the time until all butter has been absorbed into mixture. Cover cake quickly with a thin spread of mixture, after chilling runny mixture (when made) to thicken to spreading consistency. Place remainder in a small icing bag with a small ornamental pipe affixed and decorate with a few curlicues on top, around sides and at ends. Lift into an airtight, lidded, plastic box and re-refrigerate in coldest corner for 24 hours and until immediately before service. Lift out, set on dish and cut into slices with a knife dipped into hot water.

Pound Cake

We give you ¼ lb. quantities for above pudding of what is in fact 'Pound Cake'.

Ingredients:

¼ lb. sifted flour;

¼ lb. butter;

¼ lb. castor sugar;

¼ lb. shelled eggs (or two, 2 oz. eggs).

Method: Whip butter until loose and creamy. Whip in sugar and whip again until very loose and smooth. Whip in 1 egg and 1 tablespoon flour together and whip until smooth, repeat with remaining ingredients. Turn into a buttered and floured 7¾″ × 4″ × 2¼″ bun tin and bake at Gas Mark 4, middle shelf, until just springy on top (approximately 45 minutes).

GRANITA DI LIMONE (Lemon Water Ice)

This is the one which looks exactly like snow! Very refreshing.

Ingredients:

½ pint strained lemon juice;

¼ lb. castor sugar;

1 pint cold water;

2 very stiffly whipped egg whites.

Method: Place sugar and water in a thick, small pan. Set over very low heat. Allow every grain of sugar to dissolve before raising to boiling point. Bring to slow rolling boil and maintain for 5 minutes and then allow to become completely cold. Stir in lemon juice. Freeze in shallow (covered) containers, then scrape back into a bowl. Whisk down to fluid again and cut and fold in the stiff egg whites and re-freeze until required.

GRANITA AL CAFFE (Coffee Water Ice)

Ingredients:

8 oz. very finely ground coffee;   2 fl. oz. fresh boiling water;

4 oz. castor sugar;   1 pint whipping cream.

Method: Place coffee and sugar into an ordinary enamel jug and pour on the boiling water. Stand the jug in an outer container *au bain Marie,* i.e. with more boiling water poured **around** the jug in its container. Set over the lowest possible heat, so that the outer water only shivers and does not bubble. Maintain for 45 minutes. Remove jug and leave until quite cold. Then strain through a double fold of muslin lined out into an ordinary round sieve. Pour into shallow containers and freeze. When frozen except at mid-centre of containers, scrape back into a roomy bowl, whip down very thoroughly, add ½ the given cream, stir in, return to container and freeze until required. Then whip up remaining cream very stiffly indeed. Spoon frozen coffee into tall glasses until ⅔ filled. Surmount with spirals of the whipped cream and serve with long spoons and small glasses of iced water to accompany them.